D1524258

SUCK, DON'T BLOW

SUCK, DON'T BLOW

Jane Furnival

MICHAEL O'MARA BOOKS LIMITED

First published in Great Britain in 1998 by
Michael O'Mara Books Limited
9 Lion Yard, Tremadoc Road
London SW4 7NQ

A CIP catalogue record for this book
is available from the British Library

ISBN 1-85479-365-9

1 3 5 7 9 10 8 6 4 2

Designed and typeset by Martin Bristow

Printed and bound by WSOY, Finland

Contents

Acknowledgements

I would like, above all, to thank Lesley O'Mara for asking me to write this book, Gabrielle Mander for her enthusiasm and patience, and Editor, Elise Dillsworth. Also Mary Pachnos, my agent at Aitken & Stone.

Particular thanks are due to the curators and archivists who have generously shared their knowledge, showed me machines and heaved boxes of old catalogues from cupboard-tops. David Woodcock, Deputy Curator of the Secret Life of the Home at the Science Museum, London. John Narborough, Curator of the Milne Electrical Collection at Amberley Museum, West Sussex. Penny Feltham, Senior Archivist at the Museum of Science and Industry, Manchester. James Bunce of the Vintage Gas Cooker Collection, Cirencester. Philip Johnson at York City Archives. The Library staff of the National Magazine Company and the London Library, and those at the Consumers Association, Electricity Association and the Advertising Archives in London.

The company historians, too, some retired. Jim Smart of John Lewis and Jenny Webb for her work on microwave ovens kindly lent by the Institute of Home Economists, Betty Bowen and Pat Templeton at Littlewoods, Michael Peters, electrical retailer in Bedford and Susan Breakell, Company Archivist at Marks & Spencer.

Sadly, most companies have lost their archives in takeovers, fires and corporate chaos. Other companies deserve gratitude for preserving their history, among them Aga, Alessi, Dualit, Electrolux, Flavel, Kenwood, Liberty, Magimix and Vax. Press officers who have gone the extra mile to help are Rebecca Norman at Aga, Hannah Shepherd and Amanda Slaydon at Herald Communications and all at Saffron PR.

My personal thanks go to Sally Rutty for doggedly tracing many names and telephone numbers, to Alice Hart-Davis for assuring the London Library that I am indeed a proper person to join their celebrated ranks, and to all those who have shared their recollections with me, particularly food historian Ivan Day, Prue Leith, Suzanne Wilkinson (Consumer Editor of the Good Housekeeping Institute), Sylvia Smith, Yvonne Thomas, Kath Parker, Peta Flint, Debbie Brodie, Liz Jupp, Andrea Spain and Ian Fells, Professor of Energy Conversion at Newcastle University. And also to Kate for cleaning and to Noelene for doing the ironing while I wrote this book. Where would I have been without you?

Last but not least, my thanks go, too, to my husband Andy Tribble for your skill in installing and reviving old machines for us to use at home, from the brilliant Incredible Bogey coal range to that ancient Colston dishwasher that never really worked.

Author's note: Before 1970, a pound had twenty shillings, each of twelve old pennies or pence, written as *s* for shillings and *d* for pence. Some prices were in guineas, a pound and a shilling each. After 1970, the pound consisted of 100 new pence, written as *p*. One old penny was worth ½p.

Introduction

WHETHER you have treasured an old toaster with side flaps, a threadbare Hoover or a fifties fridge, or you just love old machines, this book is for you. It is also for anybody who wants to travel back through time, not to grand historical events but to daily life: to experience the rustle of lace, the chink of china and the smell of puddings which surrounded people as they worked and lived at home.

Old machines have an inherent charm. With their funny names like the Dreadnought Dishwasher and the White Mountain Potato Peeler, they are relics of a more leisured past when raisins needed de-stoning, and of a frivolous time when machines were invented to butter toast and crack eggs. They are links with a proud industrial history, when manufacturers embellished machines and made them last for years without the need for complicated repairs. This is all too rare a quality today, when a computer is considered junk if it hiccups at six months old and repair men charge high call-out fees just to say that a trivial fault is 'not worth fixing'.

Machines are empty subjects without the people who invented and used them. Within these pages you will find those larger-than-life characters and their stories. You'll meet Hubert Booth, who nearly choked to death on the dust that he sucked into his mouth to demonstrate that a vacuum cleaner should suck, not blow, as a rival machine-maker claimed; Percy Spencer, who exploded an egg over his board of directors to convince them that microwave ovens could work; Francis Bacon, who died of cold after deep-freezing chickens in snow; and all too few inventive women, like Mrs Cockran of Indiana who invented a long-forgotten dishwasher; not forgetting the nameless engineers who fiddled around in draughty rooms to perfect the Big Idea.

It is the ingenuity, persistence and grit of these people in overcoming adversity that have given us today's labour-saving devices. Their machines have improved our lives. Vacuum cleaners have stopped thousands of people dying of dust-related diseases. Gas and electric cookers have cleaned up our smoke-polluted air. Fridges and freezers have given us a huge choice of food, which microwave ovens let us cook when we want to. Washing machines have allowed us the freedom to wear what we want, when we want. Food processors have led to new styles of cooking. Most of all, all these gadgets have released millions of us from dreary, repetitive tasks, to do something more interesting and profitable instead.

Housework has been through many changes of image. In the fifties, 'houseproud' was a compliment to a woman. Then, in the first flush of feminism, it was considered shameful to want to stay at home and take a pleasure in cleaning and cooking. Now we say 'each to her own'. New French research has even found some women who actually find housework a sexual turn-on. According to manufacturers, more men do a share of housework than ever before and, as all women will testify, men are suddenly more interested when a machine is involved. This new interest and pleasure in domesticity must be down to the sheer fun and fascination of modern machines.

I have rescued and used many old machines. My favourite was a coal-burning cast-iron stove called The Incredible Bogey. Made for a railway stationmaster's inner sanctum, it was hauled down a narrow plank and installed in the houseboat which was my first real home. It taught me the joys of black-leading with Zebo and the economy and simplicity of cooking casseroles and boiling kettles on a heating stove.

Second only to the thrill of owning and using these quirky, fascinating machines is seeing them in museums. At Amberley Museum in Sussex, you can even try them out. The Secret Life of the Home at London's Science Museum is an inspirational gallery. One smell of the old gas at Manchester's Museum of Science and Industry and you understand immediately why people thought it would poison the food that it cooked.

Suck It and See

VACUUM cleaners nearly didn't happen. Their inventor almost choked to death on a mouthful of dust during an experiment in a London restaurant. Hubert Cecil Booth was checking whether dust could be sucked out of furniture effectively. He had put his handkerchief on a plush chair, put his lips against it and breathed in, with near-fatal results.

The year was 1901. Booth was a fairground wheel engineer whose curiosity had been excited by an American machine he had seen demonstrated at London's Empire Music Hall. It was intended to clean railway carriages, but it was pretty pathetic. A box topped with a bag blew air into the carpet in the hope of raising dust. The inventor fondly hoped that this would bounce off the bottom of the box and into the bag.

After the show, Booth's backstage chat with the inventor became 'heated', he recalled. 'I asked the inventor why he did not suck out the dust for he seemed to be going round three sides of a house to get across the front. The inventor . . . remarked that sucking out dust was impossible and that it had been tried over and over again without success. He then walked away.' So Booth researched the idea of a powered fan creating a vacuum which sucks dust-laden air inside a bag.

He patented his vacuum cleaner in 1901 and launched the British Vacuum Cleaner Company to market Puffing Billy, as it was called. It was an impressive horse-drawn red box on wheels, like a fire engine, tended by uniformed men who did the cleaning. The petrol-powered engine sucked dust through several hundred feet of flexible tubes, which could be passed through high windows. It cost £2,000 at today's prices, but Booth was loath to sell his machines so he hired them out.

The most fashionable houses clamoured to have the smart red vans and attendants outside, signalling to the neighbourhood that they were giving a 'vacuum tea party'. Guests sipped tea and marvelled as the long hoses were fed through the windows and the street throbbed with the engine noise. The dirt was sucked out of the carpet through a glass inspection chamber so that everybody could see the machine in action. The job cost £13, which was equivalent to the yearly wages of a tweeny – the dirty-work servant girl.

Meanwhile, those with unvacuumed carpets complained. As a result, Booth was fined hundreds of pounds for parking his machines in the street illegally, though he was found not guilty of frightening cab horses with the noise. He eventually had to take court action to establish his right to park. He was also swamped in court cases from some of the 30 other inventors who had registered vague vacuum-cleaner ideas from around 1869, which he had known nothing about. A lot of money was at stake and he had to defend the originality of his idea under cross-examination 'in no uncertain manner by the leaders of the English bar', he said later. He convinced the jury that rivals like the 'hooded broom with suction' were 'hopelessly uneconomic to work', 'hopelessly impossible' and with 'no appreciation of requirements'. As one judge pointed out to a disappointed inventor, 'this vacuum cleaner is the only one that has ever really done the work.'

One of the first carpets to be vacuumed was the great blue Coronation carpet beneath the throne at Westminster Abbey, ready for Edward VII's coronation. In 1902, Booth demonstrated the

cleaner for King Edward and Queen Alexandra, probably on an old red carpet they had knocking about. Shocked by the amount of dust that they saw whooshing through the glass inspection tube, the Royal couple bought two machines for Buckingham Palace and Windsor Castle. Not surprisingly, this proved to be a massive publicity boost. So did the vacuum cleaners bought by the French President for the Elysée Palace in Paris, German Kaiser Wilhelm II, Tzar Nicholas II and Sultan Abdul Hamid in Constantinople, not to mention Dickins & Jones department store in Regent Street, London, followed by the House of Commons.

Brighter, cleaner carpets weren't the only benefits of vacuuming. Here was an end to the annual practice of families moving out into a hotel while the servants turned the house upside down for Spring Cleaning. Now it could be done around them. A picture of that time shows an Edwardian lady in white frills sitting watching a serene maid vacuuming around her as she sips tea, a stretch of lighter coloured carpet in her wake to demonstrate the machine's marvellous effect.

The health benefits were broadcast when the Prince of Wales analysed the dust in his vacuum cleaner at Marlborough House and

found over three million live organisms. Half a ton of dust was vacuumed from a West End shop by two machines, working overnight. During World War One, an outbreak of spotted fever among Navy Volunteers was causing deaths. Fifteen vacuum cleaners removed 26 tons of dust from the girders of Crystal Palace, where it lay 6 inches deep.

London had been filthy. The new gas and electric lighting illuminated centuries of soot. Tudor floors were probably cleaner because they considered carpets too valuable to put on the floor, and kept them draped over the tables, contenting themselves with reed matting damped down with water to keep it from crumbling. But a good Victorian housewife had layers of rugs to be cleaned with an armoury of brooms. 'You had a dustpan, a long sweeping-brush, and two hand-brushes – a soft one and a stiff one,' recalled Miss Kirby, a maid at that time. 'You just got down on your hands and knees and brushed.' The technique was to sprinkle old tea-leaves over the floor in the hope that they would absorb dust, and then sweep up the tea-leaves. Actually this just raised the dust and it settled elsewhere. The advantage of having rugs, rather than carpets, was that you could pick them up periodically, hang them on the washing-line and beat the dust out with a cane carpet-beater.

Two carpet sweepers with rotary brushes – Bissell's *Grand Rapids* and the Ewbank *Royal*.

Housewives had some help after 1876, when the Grand Rapids carpet sweeper came from America. Essentially, this was a push-along box at the end of a broom handle. The box wheels turned a brush underneath. This dislodged dirt and swept it inside. Outside it looked rather grand, in walnut wood and ornate trimmings. Its inventor was

Melville Reuben Bissell, an Ohio china seller who devised it to clean up his straw-filled storerooms which gave him asthma. Soon, the Bissell company adverts boasted that his sweeper was 'in daily use in the households of HM The Queen.' Presumably, she plumped for the Parlour Queen model 'for the thickest piles' at 17s 3d. By 1910, there was a Bissell for everyone, including a Miniature for ladies to use, and a 5-inch-wide Baby for children at 9d. When aluminium, discovered in 1844, eventually replaced the wooden parts in the 1930s, it made the carpet-sweeper a light and easy way of cleaning up dirt that didn't warrant getting out the vacuum cleaner.

The vacuum cleaner had usurped the Parlour Queen for the well-off. But it was neither portable, nor cheap enough for ordinary people. Others tried to fill the vacuum this created in the market. Their smaller vacuums were more exercise machines than cleaning aids. Take the Griffith foot-operated vacuum cleaner of 1905; one maid trod two wooden pedals with her feet to create the suction, while the other wielded the hose, with its glass section idea stolen from Booth. In 1906, Booth struck back with a 'portable' vacuum cleaner for sale at 35 guineas. The Trolley Vac was not really portable, weighing a hundredweight (45.36 kilos). It was a wheel-along box with six attachments for special cleaning jobs like upholstery – a link with the past of brooms and brushes so specialist that the 'chair whisk' was the correct tool to get dirt out of chair-sides. It ran off an electric light socket, which allowed people to use the cheaper rate charged by electricity companies for lighting, rather than the dearer rate for plug-in appliances.

For the majority who didn't have electricity, hand-pumped vacuums proved popular. The Daisy Vacuum Cleaner consisted of a box with a handle, wound by a boy, with a housemaid wielding the tube. The Baby Daisy of 1904 was basically a broom handle fixed to bellows. The Star, with a larger, circular bellows outside, survived until the 1930s. In 1911, Booth produced what marketing people call a Me Too – a copy of someone else's idea – grandly called the Hand Excelsior at 7 guineas. The bellows were worked by a crank handle.

Booth had provided the Big Idea. But the person who invented home vacuum cleaners was James Murray Spangler. By rights, we should call vacuum cleaning 'spangling', not 'hoovering'. In 1907, Spangler, an asthmatic school cleaner, devised a crude portable electric vacuum, catching the dust in his wife's pillowcase tied to a broom handle and powered by an electrical motor-driven pump. He sold the idea to a relation, W.H. 'Boss' Hoover, a harness-maker who was looking around for a second business because cars were taking over from horses. In 1908, Hoover started selling the new cleaners at an exorbitant $75, and it was so successful that he pulled out of leather in 1918. Spangler retired on the well-earned results of 'Yankee ingenuity'. The Hoover reached Britain by 1912, when it cost £25 – a stratospheric sum when the average wage was 30s. (£1.50) a week. But the smart gold-etched black design caught on. It was unbeatable.

By the outbreak of war, vacuums became popular among women now working in weapons factories or in the war effort. There were

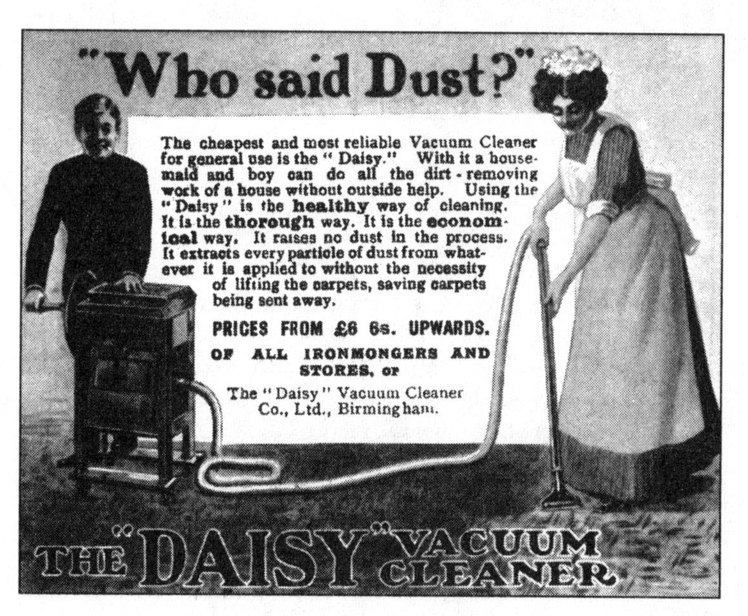

cheap machines, with names like The Improved Ferret (what did the old one do?), and there were vacuum sweepers, which were really carpet sweepers with a little extra oomph from the friction of turning wheels being pushed along very fast, like a child's toy car. There were also elaborate machines like the Siemens Vortex of 1911, which had a wall-socket in each room into which you plugged the cleaning hose, pulling the dirt into a motor in the cellar, where it kept its roar away from people.

Cylinder vacuum cleaners were the invention of Axel Wenner-Gren, a Swede who was in Vienna when he noticed a clumsy vacuum cleaner called Santo. He sneaked in to work for the company, and when he had learned enough about it, went back to Stockholm to copy and improve it. The Lux 1 was produced in Sweden in 1913 under the name Elektrolux. But you didn't lie it on the floor, as we do now. You hoisted it backpack-fashion over your shoulders using the harness provided. It was made lighter by having no brushes, relying purely on suction. Sold as a solid unit, without frills, it had a reverse action so it could be used as a paint spray.

By 1926, Booth's company, renamed Goblin, produced an upright cleaner. Hoover had introduced the famous 'Beats as it sweeps as it cleans' action which was produced using a 'beater' in the form of a cylinder behind the brush. In 1936, *Good Housekeeping* magazine made a comparison between Hoover 'now' and in 1926, commenting that 'the price of the new machine is 1 guinea less than the old one, and it has a combined motor-driven brush and beater. The hand-grip is of soft rubber. A small electric lamp is embodied in the motor-housing to light up dark corners, and the motor has two speeds.'

Catchy adverts helped Hoover. A headline recommended the benefits of 'positive agitation', illustrated by a pouting flapper pulling the machine across the ancestral carpet. Cinemas showed a musical in which a Hoover chorus line sang to the tune of 'O My Darling Clementine': 'O my carpet, O my carpet, O my carpet, don't forget – with a Hoover, yes a Hoover, we will beat the blighters yet.' There was also an army of door-to-door salesmen. One confided his secret. 'I find the wealthiest-looking house in the district, knock at the front door and pretend to the lady that my car has broken down and I am going to a hotel overnight until it's mended. I say that I don't want to leave my best Hoover in the car, and ask if she will keep it till the morning for me. I say that she is welcome to try it out. When I go back next morning, she won't part with it.'

POSITIVE AGITATION"

It pays to know the difference between The HOOVER and a vacuum cleaner

—and the dirt you HAD to harbour

Nine-tenths of house dirt is in carpets. And every woman knows that nothing will move the greater part of it but *beating*. But hand beating is difficult, laborious, disturbing. It can only be done at distant intervals. In between those beatings the embedded dirt had to stay—recognised, loathed, but harboured.

Now comes POSITIVE AGITATION, embodied in the new Greater Hoover. It is beating reduced to an exact scientific process. You can now beat your carpets far more thoroughly than by the most painstaking handwork, *as they lie on the floor*. And do it dustlessly, effortlessly, electrically, so gently that years are added to their lives.

Can any woman ignore such a discovery? When it actually enables the new Greater Hoover to get, in ordinary cleaning time, 131% more dirt from carpets than even the former Hoover – the world's recognised previous best cleaner? When it makes possible brand-new standards of home-cleanliness?

The Greater Hoover costs no more. You can buy it on the easiest of terms. Ask your Authorised Hoover Dealer to demonstrate.

A British Empire Product

The New HOOVER

It BEATS ... as it Sweeps as it Cleans

HOOVER LIMITED, 229-233 REGENT STREET, LONDON, W.1

Among other companies, a favourite ploy was to sell the vacuum as a way of keeping servants. 'Now you've this, ma'am, I'll stay,' says one haughty maid in a Siemens advert. This was optimistic. Servants were deeply suspicious. An advertisement by the artist John Hassall, headlined 'Help!', reveals the true state of affairs, as a maid seems to be running away from a vacuum cleaner. Later, he replaced it with a new headline, 'Friends'. A brilliantly ominous advert of 1925, for Western Electric, quotes a strange tale from *The Daily Express*: 'The dust off a carpet in a room occupied by a tubercular patient was collected and 48 guinea-pigs were exposed to it – 47 of them died from tuberculosis.'

By the 1930s, machines tried to compete by offering to do a lot more than just suck dirt. The Airway of 1930 also blew, to make a hairdryer. The futuristic Tellus from Sweden, 1931, was capable of drying clothes, hair, heating or fanning the room and spraying paint.

The coming of plastic made such machines lighter, and allowed them to be made in helpful shapes. General Electric's Roll-Easy was a horizontal cylinder which could roll up and downstairs. Its

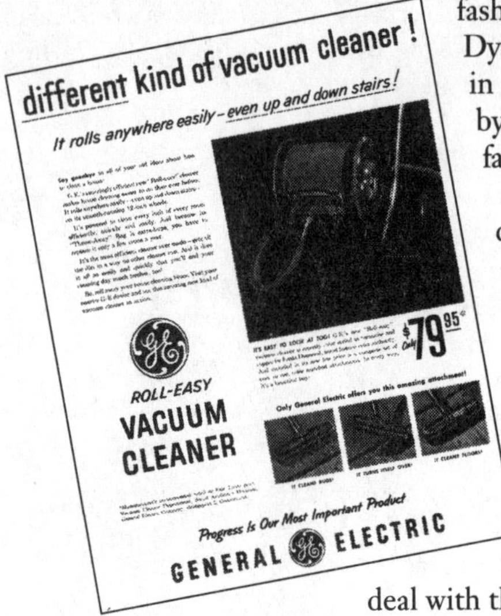

fashion-sense foreshadows Dyson, 'smartly colour-styled in turquoise and copper by Freda Diamond, noted fashion colour-authority'.

It also had a large dustbag, which needed changing less often. As users became more critical, they realized that vacuum cleaners had a problem with dustbags. As they filled, they clogged, reducing the suction power hugely. Singer tried to deal with this with a double-size bag in its Roll-a-Magic Double Capacity Cleaner, a tank-style body which looks like modern wet and dry cleaners. This was nicely designed so that its hose came out of the top, giving users 360 degrees of turning, and it claimed 'powerful cleaning action even when the bag is nearly full.'

But the best of these futuristic machines was the Hoover Constellation. This used the latest Hovercraft technology to move on a cushion of air. It seemed part of the Brave New World which the Sixties anticipated, reminiscent of the machines which gripped people's imagination when they saw mysterious balloons on TV in *The Prisoner*. It also had a stretchy hose which allowed you to reach further without moving it. 'It took everybody by storm,' recalled Jim Smart, who then worked at John Lewis. 'We couldn't get enough. But not terribly effective at the end of the day.' It was the first home machine to sell on looks, the earliest victory of form and fashion over function. The design was immortalized in pop artist Richard Hamilton's famous collage *Just What Is It Makes Today's Homes So Different, So Appealing?*

The Constellation was a fad. Most people stuck with upright cleaners. In 1973, solid plastic boxes replaced the cloth bag, which let too much dust escape. By the 1970s, fitted carpets had arrived, so people needed to clean to the end of the room. Hoover produced the Convertible, an upright vacuum with a slot-in stretchy hose advertised as 'beats-as-it-sweeps . . . and it reaches!'

We were beginning to see a rise in allergies and breathing-related illnesses such as asthma. The coal smoke pollution which choked cities in the

1870s was replaced by car fume pollution. Standards of cleanliness rose. TV commercials emphasized higher hygiene standards for anything from teeth to kitchen surfaces. In the 1970s, Alan Brazier, a technically-minded business man, left Rank Xerox to set up a company offering to wash people's carpets at home with new commercial extraction machines using water and suction. 'He found that people didn't like his vans outside their houses, advertising to the world that someone else was cleaning their carpets,' recounted his daughter Karen. So he went into commercial cleaning.

But the failure rankled. In his garden shed, Brazier searched for a machine which would allow housewives to wash deep-down dirt from carpets themselves, but without the shrinking and rotting which people complained of from wet-cleaning machines. Existing machines were complicated. They relied on a pump and a double-sprayer which sprayed cleaning fluid on to a carpet, and then went back again to extract water. Brazier wanted a simpler format than a pump, but the carpet got sodden without it. The solution was delivered by exhaust pressure and in 1977, he patented the Vax. He approached large makers hoping to sell them the licence to make it, but was rebuffed. So he sold the machine door-to-door at £199.

People were wary of this cleaner, which could clean dry, deep-clean and also suck up spills. When the salesmen told them that ordinary vacuums mainly sucked up carpet fluff, leaving 70 per cent of dirt still in their carpets, some felt that it implied that their homes were dirty. In 1983, Savacentre in Oldbury agreed to let him demonstrate it and sold 20 of them. Within two years, Vax had enough money to advertise on TV, and sold out of machines. 'People were fighting over them in the shops,' remembers Karen.

At £100 cheaper than before, Vax became the best-selling vacuum cleaner between 1987 and 1993, selling 80,000 machines a month in 1989. When the River Severn flooded near Vax headquarters, staff helped people to clear up with the Vax.

Making vacuum cleaners can be a dirty business. In 1990, the High Court declared that Hoover had infringed Vax's patent by introducing a new cleaning head. The Court heard that Hoover was one of the companies that Alan Brazier had approached with his new idea, back in 1977, with the offer of selling the manufacturing rights, but it rejected his machine, saying it would never make enough money. The companies agreed to settle out of Court for a seven-figure sum.

Meanwhile, AquaVac and Flymo, among others, had come up with tank wet and dry cleaners which would also suck up water. Unlike Vax, they didn't clean the carpet with a special fluid, but they were a godsend to people whose washing machines had flooded, or who had debris to clean up which would break the motors of ordinary cleaners.

Artists don't usually make practical inventors, barring Leonardo da Vinci; until James Dyson. In 1979, this designer-inventor was vacuuming his new house when he was struck by his cleaner's lack of suck. When he looked into it, he realized that the fault was a design flaw to do with paper dustbags. They quickly clogged up with dust, reducing suction by 70 per cent. To solve this, he sold some shares for £10,000 and spent the next five years inventing the Cyclon, the first bagless vacuum. After 5,127 prototypes, it was a stunning design, a pink upright cleaner which claimed to be three times as powerful as any other. It relied on centrifugal force. Dust was caught at speeds of over 300 kph. The residue was dealt with by a second centrifuge at nearly

the speed of sound. Where Booth had opened a window on his cleaner's workings, Dyson opened a door. Large parts were see-through, with the gubbins whirling round and dust collecting visibly in a canister to be unclipped and emptied.

Now called G-Force and displayed in the Design Museum, it became a curiosity, sold door-to-door briefly in 1983. From 1982–4, Dyson tried to interest European firms in buying the design, with all the welcome of a fox in a chicken shed. His idea would make their machines obsolescent, not to mention kill the £100-million market in replacement cleaner bags. Dyson sold the rights in America in 1984. After a year, the buyer pulled out, so Dyson took the G-Force to Japan, where it was acclaimed. Progress was halted while Dyson sued his former American licensee for patent infringement over a machine brought out after the breakup of their business relationship. After this was settled, royalties from abroad enabled him to set up a factory in Britain in 1992. Then he began making refined designs under the Dyson name here.

Dyson's Dual Cyclone machine – in both upright and cylinder form – was launched in 1993. The effect was immediate and dramatic. You could see all the dirt whisked inside, you could see Things Go Round. Suddenly, husbands and children were begging to vacuum the floor.

But there was also criticism. Some found that the filters could not cope with anything but modest house dust. There were teething problems, and a service system, antediluvian in the hard-working 1980s, of waiting long hours at home for Dyson to pick up and drop off a faulty or fixed machine. Dyson responded by publicly promising changes, and produced a visibly arty vacuum in a design-swamped age: the De Stijl, based on the Dutch modernist movement's use of intense colour-blocks. The Dyson DC01 claims to have become the best-selling vacuum cleaner ever, outselling all others by nine to one.

Dyson's newest cleaner, with its bacteria-killing filter, raised a storm about air quality and its contribution to the increase in asthma. It seemed that vacuums, invented nearly a century ago to clean up, have been blowing dust in their users' faces and causing them more and different problems. To encourage vacuum cleaner companies to produce better machines, the British Allergy Foundation awards a Seal of Approval. Every new vacuum cleaner sports filters and seals against the dust-mite, the bug which hides in carpets and makes life a medical misery. Allergy-consciousness has affected the fashion in floor coverings, away from carpets and towards less bug-harbouring wood with mats. Dual hard and soft-clean floor-machines are appearing. In 1997, Vax launched a hard floor washer-drier, the Sahara.

People have always fantasized about a robotic cleaner. Voice-activated machines, or those which automatically clean dirt they 'see' without being told to, are feasible. In 1991, Electrolux in America introduced a commercial 'robotic' cleaner for hospitals and airports. Then in 1997, it refined its ideas to produce a robot cleaner, which it plans to begin producing shortly. A smooth disc, its slimness allows it to slide everywhere including under beds, and it can navigate using radar. When placed on the floor, it will automatically start cleaning any room without help, doing the edges first. Afterwards, the owner plugs it into a recharger like a mobile phone.

Vacuum cleaners have turned from roaring monsters in the street into mechanized pets. Dyson has helped to create household machines with the most personality. Looks are vital – above performance. The latest best-selling vacuum is as specialist as the chair-whisk to the Victorians. A green plastic blob by Guzzini, The Crumb Vacuum is the tool you use to clean dinner tables.

How Our Clothes Came To Be Shaken, Not Stirred

THE greatest boost to the fashion industry has not been Chanel or Dior, but the automatic washing machine. As machines got better and faster, we could afford to change our clothes and our styles more often. But there is one distinctly unchic item of clothing which washing is responsible for adding to a woman's wardrobe: the pinafore. Pinnies were standard women's wear for centuries, put over frilled and tucked dresses to protect them from dirt so that they wouldn't have to wash them more often than necessary.

Until 50 years ago, Monday was always washday. It took the rest of the week to get clothes dry and ironed before Sunday church. That was the iron test of a woman's skill. Her family's turn-out would be mercilessly dissected by neighbours, who used the long sermon time to scan everyone's Sunday best clothes for a droopy frill or grey collar.

The earliest washing machine was a washerwoman. If you could afford to, you sent clothes to be washed by her at a laundry, or your 'treasure' would come to your home every few weeks.

In an ideal world, she would arrive before dawn, build a fire in the garden where the smoke couldn't pollute the house, and fetch 20 gallons of water to boil in a 'copper', a heavy vat housed in its own covered shed. When the water was hot, she would use the tap at the base to fill wooden tubs made from barrels sawn in half, called dolly-tubs. Clothes were put in to soak, then pounded with a dolly or peggy, which looked like a three-legged stool on a long handle. A posser, which was an early form of vacuum suction, was another aid. It looked like a cone on a handle and agitated the water by sucking it in swirls.

Stubborn stains were rubbed hard against a washboard. These wooden boards, with a ridged zinc or iron strip in the middle, appeared in the early 1800s and are still used in Norfolk. Rub too hard and you would skin your knuckles, so variations appeared, like a terrifying knuckle-duster, a hand-strap with six balls the size of marbles fitted to it over the knuckles.

After rubbing and – behind the mistress's back – scrubbing stains with a hard-bristled scrubbing brush, the washerwoman would lever and lift her washing out of the tub by winding it round a wooden 'copper stick', then tip it back into the copper for a final boil-up. The thrifty wife might make use of the hot water by popping a pudding for dinner, wrapped in a cloth, into that final rinse, giving the washing a smell that modern fabric conditioners have never managed to reproduce.

The most famous washerwoman of them all, Toad disguised in *The Wind in the Willows*, whipped up sympathy from a train driver by claiming to have a miserable time and no money. He believed her, because washerwomen were the great commuters to work of all time, travelling miles to their clients. But a good washerwoman got extra travel expenses and food while she was working. In 1922, a day's pay was 5s, with 6d for fares and up to five meals a day, which she needed to fuel her body for the heavy job. The newly-introduced government

unemployment benefit for the same year was 12s a week, so the washerwoman would be above the breadline.

If you couldn't afford a washerwoman, and you washed for yourself, a major obstacle was getting enough water. Country people used the nearest stream, slapping their clothes against a rock – so old and universal a practice that in ancient Corinth in Greece, you can see the washing stone, worn ivory-smooth by constant friction thousands of years ago.

Although water was first piped to houses on a mains system in Nottingham in 1830, many streets still shared a single tap over a century later. Rather than slopping home with heavy buckets, women took clothes to wash at their nearest pump or well. As long as the weather was good and the water plentiful, washing was a pleasantly chatty chore and the best way of coming home with lots of gossip.

If you had no convenient stone against which to slap your clothes, you could use a beetle – a ridged stick which pounded the dirt until it loosened it. Folks in Scotland had their own separate programme when it came to beetles. They were long-handled paddles, used to chase off peeping toms who hung around, eager for a glimpse of a muscular thigh as the women tucked up their skirts, got into tubs of cold water in pairs with their arms on each other's shoulders and trod on the clothes to loosen the dirt, singing rhythmic songs to help them.

Did clothes get very clean? They didn't have biological washing powders, but they did have very high standards. If something failed to come out clean, it was prudently sent to the dyers to give it a new lease of life. 'Confound the dyers! Their souls are dipp'd in scarlet sin,' wrote Jane Austen after one discouraging result. The never-ending search for whiter whites was helped in 1853, when the tax on soap was repealed.

When the first soap powder was invented in 1863, some people complained that the smell made them feel ill. They stuck to soaking clothes in old-fashioned urine, a whitener introduced by the Romans which had the advantage of being free and needing no hot water, as soap did. Until the 1890s, many poor families in the north would pool their urine in a barrel kept in their back alley, and share it out on washday. Cow dung was sometimes added to a cold water tub, although it was said to cause something ominously called The Itch.

Most people used lye, a perilously strong home-made liquid made from water boiled with ashes, which could cause skin burns or blindness.

To get whiter whites, women would 'blue' the clothes with a powder made from powdered glass and cobalt which they put in a 'dolly bluebag' and added to the water. Collars were stiffened with corn starch, a Dutch invention which made everything so notoriously uncomfortable that it was dubbed 'the devil's liquore' by Philip Stubbes in 1583.

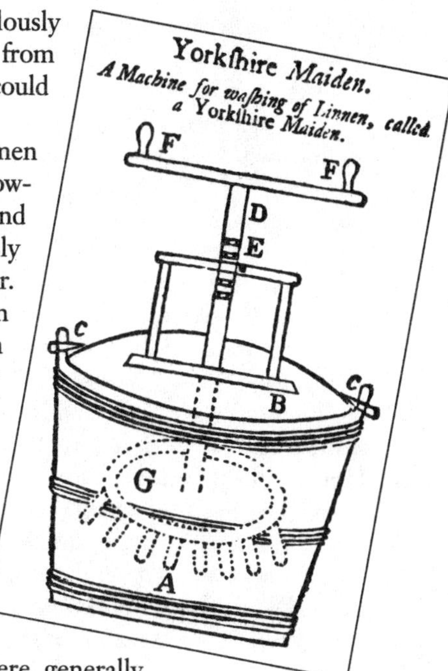

The earliest-known washing machine was the Yorkshire Maiden, named to suggest that it was a labour-saving substitute for the strong-armed northern lasses who were generally considered to be the elite of laundresses. In 1752, the *Gentleman's Magazine* mentioned that the Maiden 'has been long in use', adding that three different inventors claimed the credit for it. It is hard to see why they bothered, since it didn't offer much improvement over hand-washing, or save much labour.

It was a barrel; a slight advantage because it took more clothes than a tub. This had a lid with a handle sticking through the top. You pulled and pushed this to agitate the clothes, thus reducing your chances of getting splashed. You still had to boil hot water, and fill and empty the heavy barrel, which had no tap at the bottom to drain the water.

Machines like this were still used this century. 'Mother had a washing machine which was reasonably modern,' recalls Mrs Armstrong, brought up in Yorkshire in the 1920s. 'It was the posser type you moved backwards and forwards.' And as late as 1960, the Burlington mail order catalogue offered its direct descendant. At 12s, the 'hand-operated washer in white/red polythene' was a bucket with a lid. A handle stuck up through the middle of the lid, and was the 'agitator (with) easy up and down movement.'

In 1758, William Bailey invented the earliest 'automatic', a rotary machine that stirred clothes when you wound up a handle. Intended for use in poor houses, it was the first – and only – triple-tub machine, made up of a chorus-line of three identical wooden barrels, with three identical dollies suspended over them, joined by a horizontal rod overhead, with a handle at the end. To stir all the dollies in all the tubs together, the laundry maid had to turn the handle. It was heavy work, but with it, she could wash and rinse three batches of clothes separately at the same time.

Over the next 100 years, single-tub washing machines appeared on the handle-turning, paddle-swooshing principle. They had wonderful names like the Washerwoman's Assistant or the Housewife's Economizer of 1792. Many were souped-up with geared handles which made turning a smoother operation. Some tipped the wash barrel on its side, like a butter churn. You could take your choice, depending on whether you preferred to get backache from leaning over the top, or to pull your shoulder as you bent down to turn a handle at the side.

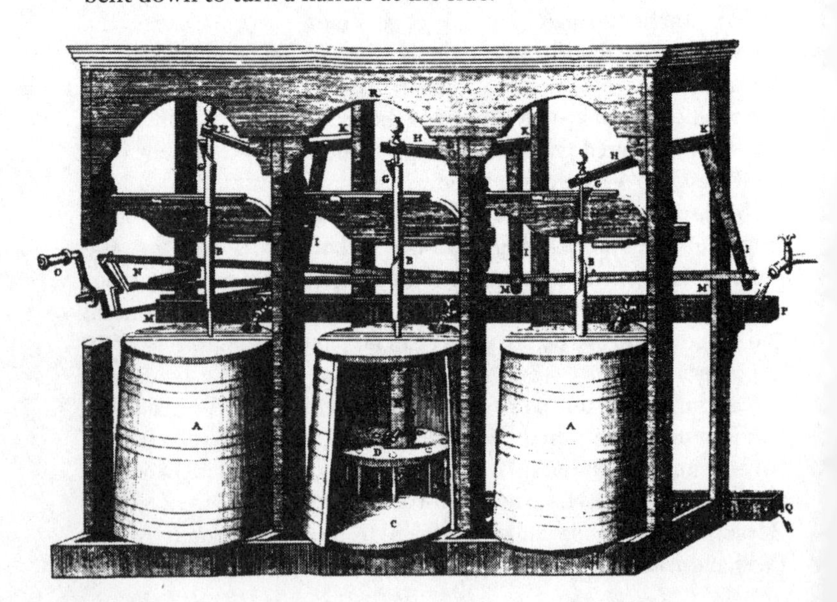

In many ways, the plain old hand-stirred dolly was better. The machines only turned one way and clothes wrapped round the dolly inside, getting tangled and torn. The problem was only solved by the Pan-American and Canadian Red Star machines in 1845, which had cog-wheels to give a twist-and-reverse action as you turned the handle, thus releasing the clothes.

Inventors had a field-day with washing machines, and all sorts of outlandish designs were tried. American inventor E.D. Wilson's 1846 effort looked like a small boat. You pumped the handle at the side to push a pendulum over a bed of rollers, sandwiching the clothes in between. This idea reached Manchester in the 1860s, where Chatterton and Bennett's Float Washer 'imitates exactly the knuckles of a vigorous washer-woman, only of course acting in a moment on a surface of clothes a hundred times as large,' says *The Journal of Domestic Appliances*. The Americans were still using the principle in 1926, when the Old Faithful Self-working washer was available by mail order to those who felt that electricity was the New Unfaithful and wouldn't last.

Washing was strictly a woman's job. Single men or widowers left with children would wash at night in secret so that they wouldn't be made fun of. But a letter to *The Lady* magazine in 1885 revealed the eternal truth that all women know about machines that do house-work: when a new-fangled machine arrives, suddenly it becomes socially acceptable for a man to operate it, even though he wouldn't be seen dead doing the same job by hand.

'J' writes: 'For years I have sent my linen to be washed in the New Forest, 100 miles into the country, for the sake of the scent that comes back to me. But the South Western Railway, with its delays and its expense, has beaten me out of this field, and my London laundress varnishes my husband's shirt-fronts (with starch) until they look like glazed paper, burns the linen in some way, loses much of it, and is altogether unsatisfactory.'

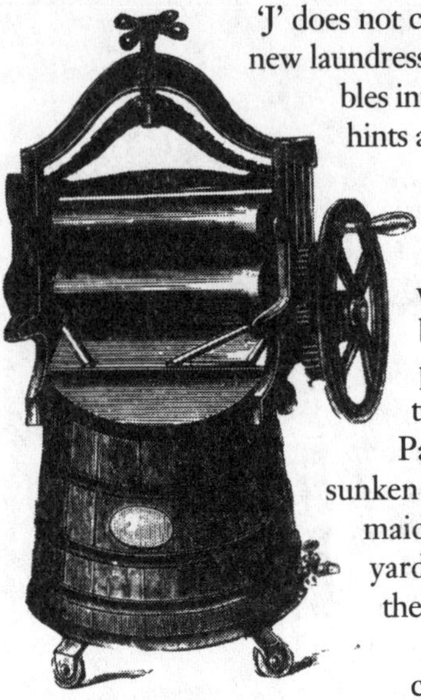

'J' does not consider the obvious solution: to get a new laundress. Instead, she decides to turn her stables into a fully-fledged laundry, and asks for hints and tips on how to go about it.

This request was blatant social climbing – only really grand houses had their own laundry. Laundries were hot to handle for any mistress, because the job of laundress attracted pretty young girls who didn't want to be subservient housemaids. At Pakenham Hall in Ireland, in 1840, a sunken passage was built to keep laundry maids from meeting the grooms in the yard while walking from the laundry to the drying area.

'Xantippe', *The Lady*'s agony aunt, clearly thinks that 'J' is going over the top, since her first tip is to recommend a good Northern laundry-maid who can come down to London for three days for 21s and her return fare. But if 'J' really wants to set up a laundry, she advises her to buy a Household or Villa Washer 'with reversing action, fitted so as to increase the speed of the Dolly by 30 per cent'. This will cost her £6 10s, with £2 15s for a mangle. She should employ a man 'to turn the washing machine' as an extra after-hours job.

This Household Washer would be one of the new heavyweight, cast-iron turning machines, the household equivalent of the massive steam trains which transformed travel and industry outside the home. Such machines weren't perfect. People forgot they needed oiling, and then complained that clothes emerged with rust spots.

There were others who thought that the churning action of a dolly was unnecessary. In 1883, Mrs Beeton recommended a machine because it was really good at doing nothing very much. The Vowel, patented in 1861 (types A, E, I, O and U) resembled a rocking cradle, lined with wooden ribs. It didn't agitate the clothes, because it had nothing inside 'which can destroy clothes in any way'.

Ironically, Mrs Beeton was right. Effective washing boiled down to hot water, good soap and elbow grease. The machines which are the ancestors of modern automatics were those which didn't stir, but simply heated their own water and turned to rub the clothes together.

Self-heating machines were patented in 1782, but J.T. King, an American laundry king, decided that any machines which used 'pounders or dashers' were barking up the wrong tree. His reasoning was more intuitive than rational. If steam was the great god that could move heavy engines for mining and trains, then surely the power of steam alone would clean clothes?

In 1851, he developed the machine that is the basis of the modern washing machine. The clothes were put in a perforated tub, turned by a steam engine for 20 minutes. But the tub didn't contain the water. This was kept in a larger, outer drum, heated by a coal fire, so that the clothes were dipped into the water as they turned. The machine used less water, because clothes were passed through the water, not soaked in it.

In 1862, Pearson & Co.'s Marvellous Steam Washer copied the same idea in a neater casing. The water was heated by a slim but ineffectual-looking tray of charcoal or gas beneath the drum, and its advertisements showed a little girl turning its handle. A picture of a smiling child, or the phrase 'so easy that a child could do it', cropped up repeatedly in advertisements for new home-help machines. They must have had some pretty strong-armed children in those days.

Others had different ways of making the machine look like a money-saving idea. The Economic Cooker/Wash Boiler of 1888 had a single high-gas burner. It was a cast-iron box which heated water. When you had finished your washing, you lifted the boiling pan out and slotted oven doors inside instead.

The first electric washing machine was invented in 1909. John Fisher, an American, fitted a motor on top of a hand-operated washing machine so that it would turn the hoops that turned the handle. This was a mixed blessing. Either the motor gave out because it was splashed, or it gave the user electric shocks. It didn't heat the water, nor pump it out, so there was still the hassle of filling, heating and emptying water.

Miele, a German company, was set up in 1899 by Carl Miele and Reinhard Zinkann to produce industrial dairy equipment. It began making butter churns in 1901 and used the same basic design, a small oak tub with an agitator, to make washing machines. The idea took off so well that they stopped making churns. By 1914, they were making 12 different washing machines, including new electrical and water-driven washing machines.

But it was Thor from Chicago which conquered all. In the same year, it launched a motorized washing machine in sparkling enamel, with the motor safely under the box, complete with powered wringer and plug. It would work from a light fitting overhead and cost a penny in electricity per wash. 'The whole of the week's laundry can be washed, wrung and made ready for drying within the hour,' claimed Thor's British advertisement.

The whole week's laundry? Even allowing for advertising puff, this made an interesting point. Until recently, people were smellier. When electric washing machines first appeared, people weren't used to washing their clothes so often because it was such hard work.

The idea of washing as we do, not because something is dirty but to freshen it at the end of a day, hadn't occurred. Instead, they wore clothes for days. 'A certain clever housekeeper' boasts in *Good Housekeeping*, March 1922, of her 'much prized' electric washing machine in which she washes everything 'that is at all soiled'.

They stuck to dark colours which showed less dirt, and a lot of heavy wool, which absorbed personal smells. In the days before deodorants, women stitched dress shields under their arms and removed and washed those rather than the dress.

They wore shirts and dresses which they didn't wash for a week or more, with detachable white collars and cuffs which could be changed and washed more easily and cheaply. Instead of buying a new shirt, men bought new collars by the dozen, fixed on with irritating tiny collar-studs. The less well-off, and bachelors, avoided washing by wearing cheap, scratchy wipe-clean collars made of celluloid, an early stiff plastic. Flora Thompson, in her memoir of country life early this century, *Lark Rise to Candleford*, described being covered with grease for warmth, then sewn into her vest, an undergarment which was expected to stay on all winter until her mother unpicked the stitching.

BUY A
SUNRISE
PATENT
WASHING
MACHINE

IT REDUCES TOIL,
SAVES TIME,
WASHES CLOTHES AS
IF WASHED BY HAND

IT IS VERY CHEAP. PRICE £4 10 0

Order or write for further particulars to—

THE SUNRISE SPECIALITY CO., LTD.
262 Holloway Road, LONDON, N.17

Telegrams: "Pertaining, Holway, London."
Telephone: 1636 North.

Even the very rich were careful not to create more washing. In 1936, the novelist Dorothy L. Sayers described her heroine Harriet Vane buying a black mourning dress for the death of King George V – with ten white collars so that she could wear a fresh one with it each day, presumably without washing the dress. And Harriet was married to the millionaire Lord Peter Wimsey and had a personal maid.

Women really started buying washing machines in Britain after World War I. Servants became scarce and expensive. 'To-day,' bewails Adam Gowans-Whyte in 1922's *Good Housekeeping* magazine, 'a servant costs in wages, food, laundry and breakages (to say nothing of moral and intellectual damage) about £100 a year.' In 1900, there was one servant per 15 households. By 1950, this had changed to one per 42 households.

If you wanted to hang on to a good maid, you had to lighten her load and buy a machine. Adam Gowans-Whyte rattles on about the problem. '"No washing" is the first law of domestic service nowadays, and the capable visiting washerwomen of an earlier generation seem to have become extinct. The alternative to home washing is the laundry, with its high prices, its irritating losses and delays.'

Laundries had other surprises in store, as Lilly Frazer observed in a chatty guide to housework for the middle-class woman called *First Aid to the Servantless*, 1913. 'Often the laundress's children wear the garments during the week. I would rather do anything than allow children of mine to be exposed to the infection thus frequently created.' Then there were other darker ideas, like the prejudice sewn by the movies that Chinese laundries might be centres of the white slave trade, carrying young European girls off to a fate worse than death . . .

If you decided to dispense with a maid or a laundry, you suddenly realized how difficult washing was and bought a machine to help you. Washing machine makers vied to capture the imagination with gimmicks, or a scientific-sounding name, even if the machine did largely the same thing as before. What is curious is that machines that could turn themselves electrically didn't also use electricity to heat the water. Krauss's coal-fired washing machine of 1923 had a closed tub for clothes which looked like a giant perforated pepper pot. If the electric motor could turn it within a drum of water, it seems an extra bother to have to light a coal fire underneath it, too.

Thor built on its success by introducing Thor Automagic, a washing machine which doubled as a dishwasher. Then it tweaked its machine again and advertised 'lifters' which pulled the washing out of the water and put it back. In 1922, the Sun Electrical Company fought back by offering a washing machine which did this – and more. Its advertising in the pages of *Good Housekeeping* manages to combine a snide dig at Thor with a promise that is the all-singing, all-dancing equivalent of Hoover's 'beats-as-it-sweeps-as-it-cleans' advertising promise for vacuum cleaners. 'Some electric washers lift and dip the soiled fabrics. And it is a good method. Other electric washers rock and toss the soiled fabrics to and fro. The ABC Super Electric washer does both.' So there.

Vacuum cleaners were all the rage. Some washing machine makers jumped on the bandwagon and offered 'vacuum washing'. The Pioneer 'Tip-Top' was advertised around 1910 as a 'vacuum chamber'. It wasn't. It was actually a wooden box with a louvred paddle which, according to the sales brochure, swung 'largely by its own momentum', implying 'not by your elbow-grease, Mrs Buyer', though it must have been pretty feeble. 'The movement of the handle sets up a powerful suction in the vacuum wash-box, which extracts every particle of dirt from heavy blankets to delicate lace curtains.'

The vacuum Dolly was the same sort of thing, for those who wanted the latest technology in a hand-washing form. It was a new form of the posser, a metal sink plunger lookalike which sucked dirt out of fabric, but it sent *Good Housekeeping* into ecstasies in 1922. A photograph showed a woman in a head-dress halfway between a nurse and a nun, severely punishing a bowl of clothes with it.

Even more elaborate was a machine posser, the 1935 Magic Vacuum Cup Washer, boasting three washing cups which reproduced the action of the hands. This conjures up a picture which is pure Heath Robinson.

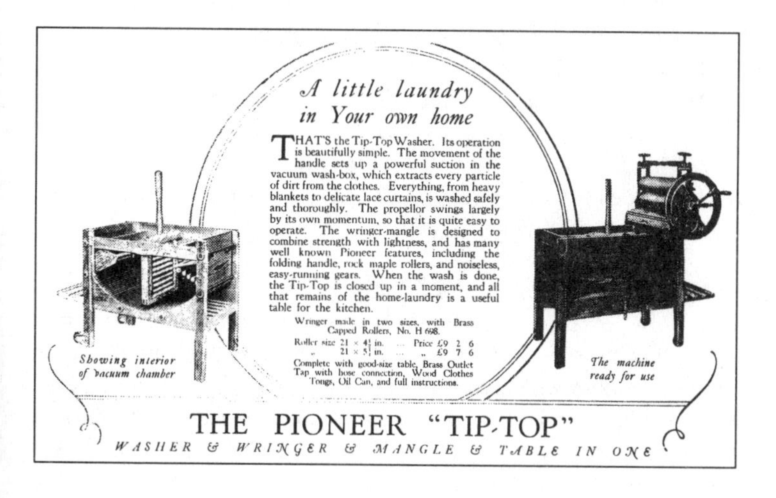

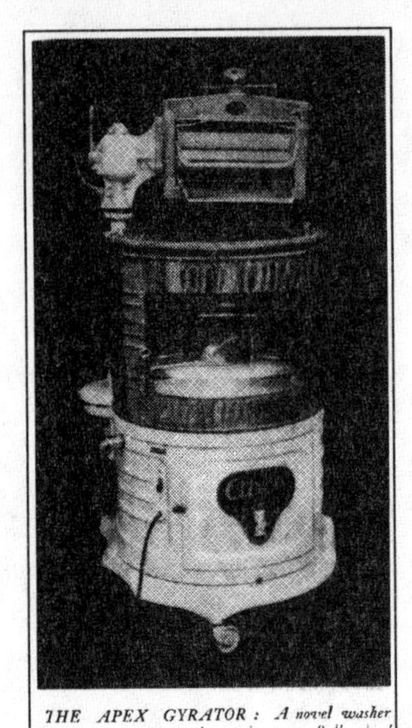

THE APEX GYRATOR: A novel washer which is guaranteed to clean an 8-lb. load (thirty pillow-slips or sixty towels) in five to eight minutes

By the 1930s, Hotpoint had produced yet another impressive, scientific-sounding name for an electric dolly, a 'gyrator' (a word taken from the poet Yeats, who used the word gyre to describe whirly things). In 1936, Apex-Vactric claimed to be 'years ahead' with 'the double-dasher', a figure-of-eight-shaped agitator which, for some reason, was supposed to 'coax out dirt gently and thoroughly' but probably sent it scurrying for cover.

In 1937, Herbert Brothers of West Hartlepool drew a deep breath and hoped to cover all the fancy ways of moving clothes through water, with the 'Easy' range of washing machines. 'Purchasers are offered a choice of three different cleansing actions – the vacuum cup, the Spirolator (in which, as its name implies, the agitator is in the form of a spiral), and the Turbolator, a new method which aims at providing effective washing the whole way up the tub by the use of specially curved agitator vanes.'

People had high expectations of their costly new machines. They were fuelled by advertising illustrations like that of the Western Electric Washer and Wringer in the 1920s. Under the headline 'Electrical hands that wash clothes', the picture shows a fluffy woman stuffing a frilly eiderdown into a mechanical box ridiculously too small.

These were the days before advertising had to be truthful. 'Makes clothes last longer too!' says The Sun Electrical Company of its ABC Washer gleefully. As a student in 1982, Penny Feltham found her lodgings in a converted stable block were fitted with a similar machine: a barrel with a motorized paddle in the middle. 'The machine had no hot water supply, and we had only a cold tap, so we had to carry hot water from the house in 10 gallon buckets,' she recalls. 'You put in as many clothes as you could, with washing powder. The agitator was vicious. It used to catch the clothes and rip them.

'Because there was no timer, you played both sides of an LP – about 45 minutes to time it – then turned it off. Often the machine wouldn't empty, so you put the rubber filling hose into the dirty water and sucked it until vacuum action got it to work – or you got a mouthful of dirty soapy water!

'After that, you refilled the tub with cold water and agitated it again to rinse it. You had to suck the water out again, refill and repeat. Finally you put the clothes through the wringer, trying hard not to catch your fingers.'

The massive marketing machine which backed the electricity industry did its utmost to create a need. The Sun Electrical Company hammered on about cost-savings for a household of three adults and two children, if they invested in the ABC Super-Electric Washer and Wringer in *Good Housekeeping*, 1922. 'With a washerwoman the

ELECTRICAL HANDS THAT WASH CLOTHES

YOUR washing is the same problem every other housewife is facing today. Either it's hard on you to get your washing done, or it's wearing on your clothes. Most likely it's both.

The solution is the—

ONE of the HANDS IN THE HOME

Western Electric
Washer and Wringer

ASK YOUR DEALER ABOUT IT

expenses were: washerwoman, one day, 5s, fares 6d, food 2s 6d, soap 9d, Lux 7d, Hudson's 2d. Total 9s 6d, excluding the cost of fire for copper. The ABC Super-Electric Washer and Wringer costs: Lux 7d, Hudson's 1d, Electricity 2d. Total 10d.'

But the reality was that not everybody could afford the new machines. Nor was everyone was connected to electricity, nor running water. The spread of electricity was gradual, like the spread of cable TV today. Not until 1926 was there a National Grid, a general supply – and piped water was a patchy system over the country. None of these machines were plumbed in, so the woman had to drag it over to the sink and put the hose in. If it slipped out, it deluged the kitchen floor with suds.

Meanwhile, less well-off Americans, whose electricity system was standardized faster than Britain's, rushed to buy bolt-on motors to electrify old hand-rotating machines. The price of an electrified washing machine dropped from $150 in 1926 to $29.95 in 1936 – the same phenomenon we saw in the 1980s with computers.

If you didn't have electricity, there were ingenious machines which you could use on the top of a gas stove. A good try from the pages of *Good Housekeeping* in 1922 was the Sprite Automatic Home Laundry. 'I simply love my Sprite,' says the lady owner, displaying her delicate lace nightdress fresh from the boiling water of a four-legged tub with a sort of mushroom device spouting water like a fountain in the middle. She must have asbestos hands. The advert claims that 'dirt is coaxed out of the meshes of the fabric instead of being pushed or forced out by rubbing or friction.' It means that this is a copper tub with a percolator action. Water is heated at the base and boils until it is forced up the chute in the middle.

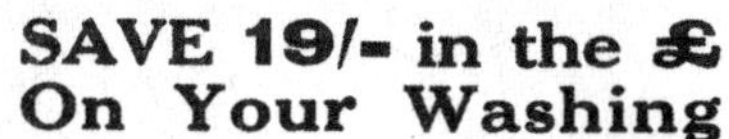

Wonderful Invention Which Does All the Work of Washing WHILE YOU REST

The "Sprite" Automatic Home Laundry is a supremely clever, practical Invention which does Household and Personal Washing without any hand labour as effectively as the finest French Laundry, but at a cost of only about **1s.** for every **20s.** charged by a Laundry.

The "Sprite" Automatic Home Laundry requires no fixing. Occupies small space. Anyone can use it. Simply put in water, soap powder, and whatever articles are to be washed. Light the gas jet and leave the "*Sprite" to do all the rest* perfectly without slightest injury to daintiest garments. Thus linen, etc., lasts twice as long.

The secret of this "SPRITE" Invention as a Home Laundry is that by an ingenious but simple arrangement within the "SPRITE" the dirt is coaxed out of the meshes of the fabric instead of being pushed or forced out by rubbing or friction.

SEVEN DAYS' FREE TRIAL

So remarkable is the success of the "SPRITE" that you are invited to try it for a week entirely at the manufacturers' risk, for the full price paid will be refunded without question on return of the "SPRITE" within seven days.

The "SPRITE" is made in sizes to suit all requirements from the price of 45/-. It requires no special fixing. Is so simple a child can use it.

Demonstrations are given daily between 9.30 a.m. and 6 p.m. (Sats. 9.30 to 1) at 42 Berners Street, Oxford Street, London, W., to which ladies are flocking and are delighted to see how effectively and easily all their washing-day troubles are solved.

DESCRIPTIVE CATALOGUE SENT FREE

Every thrifty person should write to-day for *Full Descriptive Catalogue, which contains most instructive and valuable information upon easy washing-at-home methods, and which will be sent Free on application to*

MULTICOOKER INVENTIONS, Ltd.
(Room 53), 42 Berners St., Oxford St., London, W.1

You could say goodbye to washday worries – and your knee-length silk Directoire knickers – in the clutches of the Clensic Automatic Washer, 12s 6d in 1922. This was a two-skinned tub with a pipe sticking up through the centre. You put it on your gas ring, and the hot water bubbled out through the pipe at the top and circulated on to the clothes. 'Just put the things in and take them out – as white as snow,' claims the advert. 'The CLENSIC does its marvellous work by creating a continuous flow of boiling soapy water and steam through and through the tiniest meshes of any fabric, drawing out every trace of dirt without any risk or injury.' In other words, it works by boiling.

The first fully automatic machines, which would fill, heat, empty, rinse and spin, appeared in 1930 in America. They weren't seen in Britain until the Bendix arrived in 1937. This was one of the first pressed steel, mass-produced machines. Although expensive, it should have been cheap, being turned off the production line rather than hand-built, like the old wooden washers.

Like fridges, the Bendix paid homage to the 'streamlined moderne' 1930s look inspired by the architect Le Corbusier, the Terence Conran of his time, with his cubist houses with severe straight lines softened with perfect curves. The Bendix white steel streamlined front-loader made everything else look old-fashioned. Especially the top-of-the-range £25 Hotpoint BTH electric washer in blue enamel chosen for George V's Jubilee House (a sort of Ideal Home) only a year before. Other models brought out the same year, like Beatty Brothers' 'Coronation', looked like a metal dustbin with coloured legs by comparison.

Fashions had changed, and the Bendix was a machine to match them. Women wore 'art silk', named to make the new artificial nylon sound classy. It was crackly on the skin but so much cheaper. In 1932, 10s bought three pairs of silk stockings, but seven of art silk. For dresses, new rayon fabrics appeared like the seductively-named Courgette, one of a series of materials for which Courtaulds spent £135,000 on publicity. No relation to the vegetable.

There were tantrums at home when ignorant mums boiled their daughter's new man-made fabric dresses. Man-made fabrics were notoriously prone to shrivel. This new Bendix was the first machine that could heat water without boiling it, offering a warm wash. Its makers trumpeted the benefits of a constant flow of water to the machine for 'a more hygienic wash', and its cheeseparing virtues: it used a fifth of the soap taken by other machines. It had no exposed moving parts and switched itself off after spinning. More important than any of these, one suspects, was the design with a glass window in the front door – that vital accessory which spelled success for vacuum cleaners too. People needed to see a machine working before they would believe it.

The Bendix sold to women who could afford to read the advertising in *Vogue*, then go to Harrods and buy a rayon dress. To the majority, Bendix must have seemed like something from a futuristic fantasy. The most they could hope for on a machine were adjustable legs, so that they wouldn't get backache leaning over it.

Which washing machines did ordinary women buy? The Littlewoods catalogue for 1932 gives a snapshot of the options. £2 buys the Washwell table-wringer – a wringer with a rustless tank for boiling clothes. Its one feature is a detachable plug to drain the water. Even more of a staple is 'This Complete Washing Set for an Easier Wash-Day', a set which catalogues carried until the 1960s. Just £1 buys a galvanized washing tub, small bath and hand-bowl, copper posser, Northern Queen zinc washboard, mop (presumably for cleaning up the slopped water), length of clothes line and three dozen clothes pegs. Bear in mind that a factory worker earned £1 a week and a typist £3 10s a week around this time.

By 1936, the year before the Bendix automatic, the range had increased. The slightly posher could spend their pound on a 10-gallon boiler with a gas jet and length of tubing for connecting the gas, a 'tin lading can' (looks like a tankard), and a short posser, now rechristened 'vacuum washer', the lid of the boiler ridged to double as a washboard.

Through the 1930s and 40s, inventions first considered by the Victorians, like timers, on and off switches, automatic water pumping and drying, became affordable realities. The cost of machines halved. *Good Housekeeping* in 1936 shows a top-loading 'electric servant' which it says is £6 15s – half the price of an old hand-cranked machine of 10 years before.

Washing machines could only be as good as the soap they used. The 1930s was the era of the first organized scientific research and development departments in companies. Because of the efforts of Lever Brothers and Procter & Gamble, washing powders got better. So did the cunning of the advertising copywriter. An advert for the new Persil 'oxygenated' soap powder depicts a man scolding his unfortunate wife: 'I can't think why you don't get your frocks to look as bright as Joan's – you've had enough washing experience.'

Like washing machine makers, Persil used a pseudo-scientific way of explaining the very ordinary process by which soap cleans. 'Out of Persil soapsuds come millions of eager oxygen bubbles – stirred to action by the very dirt itself! This cleansing oxygen clusters round the dirt – making it vanish right out of existence.' The phrases remind one of biological powders in TV commercials of the 1970s gobbling up the 'understains'.

The 1939 catalogue of L.G. Hawkins announces 'the most beautiful and serviceable laundry-unit in washing machine history.' Beauty is in the eye of the salesman, but 'Universal Electric Washers and Damp Driers' were certainly different – the first twin tubs. 'A complete laundry unit – a washer that spotlessly washes clothes and a dryer that needs but a minute to spin them damp-dry,' it explains. 'Will dry one load while washing another . . . Its added features and conveniences warrant your inspection.' The dryer, it goes on to say, doubles as a rinse tub and the machine is self-emptying.

In the sculleries of most homes, the simplest machine was the most popular. The old copper had become electrified and streamlined, and emerged as the Baby Burco Boiler. You filled it. It boiled. It pumped out water through a spout at the bottom – you had to remember to put a bowl next to it or disaster struck. In later models, it drained through a plastic hose which you draped over the sink. You could get a plain cylinder, but if you wanted a 'streamlined' boxy version, it cost much more – 10 guineas from Littlewoods in 1951. Littlewoods also offered a gas boiler – 'no need to light a coal fire just to get water for washing clothes,' it explained to those poor souls who hadn't yet caught up with gas and electricity.

The Second World War put paid to the idea of a regular Monday wash. Disrupted lives gave everybody an enormous reason to get a washing machine. Women were working, and washed clothes whenever they could. 'In these days of emergency, when heavy washing such as A.R.P. wear, overalls, etc. must be done at short notice, the Hotpoint is a wonder of speed and effortless efficiency,' gasped an advertisement in Spring 1940 in *The Electrical Age*, the magazine of the Women's Electrical Association.

After the war, women were not going to go back to washing with a copper. They had survived the deprivations of the war and expected, somehow, a better life to materialize amid the chaos of bombed cities. The phrase 'a return to gracious living' was bandied about in newspapers to describe a lifestyle which included spending less time at home, and going out, wearing more clothes and prettier ones now that clothing rationing had finished.

UNIVERSAL
Electric Washers and Damp Driers

A combined equipment—one compartment washes, while at the same time, the other compartment damp dries the complete tubful, ready for hanging and ironing, without each piece having to be individually passed through a wringer. Time is saved—the things are dried—buttons and fastenings cannot be damaged.

Model No. E1760 is extensively used by Convents — Institutions — Small Hotels — Large Households—wherever a laundry problem exists "UNIVERSAL" is the most efficiently known solution.

Full Specifications, etc., on request.

WASHER-DRYER
No. E1660B

A complete laundry unit—a washer that spotlessly washes clothes and a dryer that needs but a minute to spin them damp-dry. Will dry one load while washing another. The most beautiful and most serviceable laundry-unit in washing machine history. Its added features and conveniences warrant your inspection. Complete rinsing may be done in dryer basket. Self-emptying tub. Capacity both tubs 12 lbs. Finished in Jade Green.

GENERAL INFORMATION—One piece porcelain enameled tubs, dome-shaped. Triple vane agitator. Damp-proof oversize motor. Direct drive transmission. Self-emptying pump. Pump silencing valve. Safety switch. Height over all 37 in. Floor space 23x39 in. Height to edge of tub 34⅛ in. Tub size 21x15 in. Weight 202 lbs. Weight crated 250 lbs.

WASHER-DRYER
No. E1760

A large capacity washer and dryer. Oversize, rust-proof copper tub, lined with nickel. Powerful centrifugal dryer that operates independently. Washes everything, dainty silks, heavy corduroys, even rag carpets. A wonderful time and labor saver, sold with UNIVERSAL'S unqualified guarantee. Capacity both tubs 16 lbs. Finished in Green Lacquer.

GENERAL INFORMATION—Triple vane dome-shaped agitator. Damp-proof oversize motor. Direct drive transmission. Self-emptying pump. Safety switch. Height over all 42 in. Floor space 25x41 in. Height to edge of tub 37 in. Tub size 23x17 in. Weight 208 lbs. Weight crated 282 lbs.

The new clothes were a reaction against the skimpy, easy-to-wash dresses of the war, and the Make Do and Mend attitudes which made fashions in clothes move so slowly. Shops like Wallis and C & A copied Dior's New Look, the big hips and padded shoulders and calf-length skirts worn famously by Princess Margaret to Glyndebourne in 1947. The first faint stirrings of feminism could be heard in a publicity film by the Electrical Development Association called *How to Sell your Husband a Washing Machine*, a small gem of cinematic art starring Jack Hulbert and Cicely Courtneidge.

'Your husband would cut a sorry figure if he had to do your work for a day,' trills Miss Courtneidge, and the two proceed to change sex-roles in an innocently funny way. She strides home from work in a manly fashion wearing a beret, to find 'his knuckles raw through scrubbing on a washboard'. No, he whinges, he certainly won't go out to the pictures with her – his perm has fallen out and he hasn't had time to do his hair.

'I can't bear to see them lovely hands all ruined,' she announces. So off they go to the washing machine showroom. Here a tightly-belted beauty in New Look skirt and blouse wows us with the news that 'there are many reputable makes' of washing machine. Glancing homage is paid to the fully automatic washing machine, but this, it's implied, is beyond Cicely and Jack's finances, even with weekly payment credit thrown in. Then the saleslady indicates another new machine. 'This machine has a device you may not have come across before. It dries the clothes not by wringing, but by extracting the water by spinning.'

Post-war washing machines were elaborated versions of the boiler. In 1947, Hoover created one of the earliest automatic top-loaders by taking a boiler and adding an 'impellor', a water-stirrer patriotically named to call to mind the propellors used by our brave boys during the Battle of Britain. 'The impellor was built into the side of the machine to circulate the water, but it tangled the clothes,' recalls Jim Smart, who sold washing machines from the 1950s to the 1980s in a John Lewis department store. 'Hotpoint had an upright impellor, which was better. It swirled the clothes backwards and forwards.'

These same old actions were advertised in the snazzy washing machine publicity language which year by year, invented words like 'gyrafoam' and 'live water action' to describe the normal foaming action of soap and water.

Top-loading automatics had a bigger tub than front-loaders. They emptied themselves with a pump when the wash was finished. But to do it, they used a huge amount of water and electricity for heating, filling and emptying the tub three times. They spun-dry, but the loads came out still wringing wet because they could only manage around 800 rpm (revolutions per minute). Any faster and they would have turned into a heavy guided weapon, vibrating across the floor.

In 1957, Hoover launched the twin-tub. This was the same idea as the Universal back in the 1930s, but instead of green enamel tubs and clunky motors, the new machines were smartly packaged in white steel boxes, which hid all the workings neatly.

Few machines around the home have inspired such affection and loyalty as the twin-tub. Women loved them: they were controllable and easy to operate. There was a switch for the water heater, and an on/off switch, which meant that like the old coppers, women could turn the machine off to check the washing half-way through. When the washing finished, they didn't have to wring it, but could swap it to the spin dryer. As they held a hose over the sink, they could tell how much water was coming out and decide for themselves when to stop spinning. 'Twin-tubs would boil, which is what the women were after,' says Jim Smart. 'Before the war, they were brought up to boil their clothes, and they didn't think soap powders would remove the dirt.' Soap powders were among the first to advertise on television, to convince them otherwise. Omo gave away a plastic daffodil with every pack – the single most successful marketing trick, above every possible claim to do with how well the powder worked.

It was a flamboyant entrepreneur called John Bloom who laid the foundations for the mass-market in modern washing machines. He sold his twin-tub, the Rolls Washing Machine, door-to-door and became a millionaire. He bought out the fridge makers Prestcold, but after a new line of automatic front-loaders didn't sell well, he went bankrupt and left for America. When the machines he left behind broke down or wore out, women couldn't bear the idea of going back to their deserted coppers, so they went to the shops to buy a new washing machine.

Fully automatic front-loading machines were regarded with suspicion when they reached the shops in the late 1960s. They were considered uncontrollable, over-complicated and likely to break down. You put your wash-load inside, and the machine locked it in as you set a mysterious-sounding 'programme' which you couldn't alter half-way through, even if you saw colours running through the glass porthole. Newspapers carried stories of kittens trapped inside, who miraculously survived being spun at 800 rpm.

Once again, Bendix took the lead, returning to making its sideways, tumble-action washing machine after making aircraft during the War. It was followed by Maytag, Frigidaire and Washington: expensive, American machines. Ordinary people saw them at the new Launderettes which were springing up in every town. Do-it-yourself versions of the old laundries with friendly names like the Posh Wash became meeting places, new versions of the old social Mondays by the pump a century before. Working women and men could also use them as an old-fashioned laundry, dropping off the clothes and asking the attendant for a 'service wash' for a few pence.

Young singles became familiar with front-loaders at launderettes, and when they married, they felt comfortable with the new cheap Hotpoint front-loaders in the kitchens of their smart little estate houses.

The 1970s housewife had changed. As a teenager in the 1960s, she wore jeans which weren't washed for weeks as a matter of pride, and throwaway paper dresses and paper knickers as a sign of rebellion against conformity, which included doing the washing. Now this woman had grown into Superwoman. 'Ask for everything!' urged *Cosmopolitan* magazine, and in her life's balancing act which included job, home, husband and children, she didn't want to stand over a machine supervising her washing. Sheets were coloured; shirts were drip-dry Bri-nylon, and clothes were no longer a source of pride, to be boiled and checked for whiteness. She had grown up with machines in the kitchen, and they were no longer a source of wonder or worry. She just wanted to bung her washing in the machine and bring it out clean. That was the recipe for being a good mother. The Persil adverts told her so.

Washing machine makers began to work closely with washing powder companies. As a result, automatics shrunk to kitchen-size with the help of new suds-free powders which did away with the need for tubs to be large enough to hold the classic full-to-the-brim bubbles of old-fashioned soap flakes like Lux.

But problems occurred when soap bubbles welled out of the machine portholes. People didn't understand that they had to use the new powders because there wasn't room for all those bubbles in the tubs. They didn't like using them because they suspected that they didn't work. Made from oils rather than traditional fats, to start with, they produced no soap lather at all – and how could anything clean clothes, if it didn't produce bubbles? Supermarkets refused to stock them – in Spring 1975, 'twin-tubs are still a popular type of washing machine' said *The Electrical Age*. The shops that sold the front-loaders had to sell automatic powders. Eventually, the washing powder companies added back some soap. The campaign to Bring back the Bubble had succeeded.

Washing machines and washing powder companies became dependent on each other. The front-loading machines' churning and turning was seen as 'harsh' to clothes, and fabric conditioners were introduced to coat fibres with a shiny, bulking agent, putting back the 'bounce' which detergents took out. In turn, washing machines had to make extra space for them inside the detergent dispensing drawers.

The Hoover Keymatic front-loader in the 1970s was cleverly designed to form a familiar link with launderette machines. It was the first machine with an element of playfulness. You put a snazzy red keyplate into a slot in the machine, which programmed the wash. Soon, Servis and Hotpoint front-loaders were joined in the shops by the cheaper Italian makes, Indesit and Zanussi. 'The big problem with the early machines,' assesses Jim Smart, 'was that they had low spin-speeds which didn't really dry clothes. You

bought a spin dryer too.'

In an effort to counteract that, the Hotpoint 1300 appeared – and fell into the trap of being too advanced. Its spin speed of 1300 rpm produced clothes that were so dry that they could be worn immediately. But the machine shot across the room while it was spinning. The problem of dancing washing machines was not sorted out until the late 1970s, when machines had adjustable speeds of 500 to 1200 rpm.

The washer-dryer was a late 1970s attempt to suit smaller kitchens. At first, they were very slow: two and a half hours for a washing programme. People didn't like to leave the house while it was working, because there was always the risk of its overheating and causing a fire. Washer-driers developed a bad name for frequent breakdowns which, according to a Consumers' Association survey of 1996, they still have. Sometimes this was because people expected the machine to dry the same weight of clothes as it washed. But tumble drying needed more space. They had to learn to remove half the wash and dry in batches.

Front-loaders used less water than any other kind of machine. In the early 1980s, makers faced a huge backlash against machinery, which was seen as wasteful of water and power. Makers became unpopular for other reasons. Consumer groups during the recession highlighted the profit-motive which made them produce front-loaders with 'built-in obsolescence', timed to break down just outside their guarantee period. One large maker deliberately restructured the washing machines so that the bearings on the drum – the tiny supports which wear out, and are cheap and easy to fix – were welded to the drum, and could not be changed without the whole drum being replaced at £80.

Even shops were unhappy. Profits had been so pared that one major chain was known to make its money not by selling the machine, but by adding on an expensive repair warranty which the customer was panicked into buying.

The lowest point for the washing machine industry was the public humiliation of Hoover. It had sold washing machines with an offer of free airflights which had been taken up beyond its wildest predictions. It couldn't cope with the demand – and after appalling publicity, Hoover pulled out of the European washing machine market, selling its name.

People had other worries, which made them demand better, more economic machines. As water boards were privatized, water meters made people more aware of their kitchen machines' water consumption because they had to pay for it.

Each new washing machine used less water. Zanussi – whose image as a technical leader was created by the advertising slogan 'The appliance of science' – produced a jet system, spraying water through the tub on to the clothes. Automatics introduced quick wash programmes, and powder companies produced liquid and compact powders, all with the explanation of 'ecology and economy'. The backlash against biological powders saw new all-natural washing powders, billed as biodegradable, to the fury of powder giants who claimed that their enzymes broke down quickly in the environment.

The Hotpoint Ultima, displayed in London's Design Museum, demonstrates how the simple technique of washing clothes is still dressed up with scientific-sounding processes in an attempt to impress customers. It boasts 'Infobubble display', 'multi wash programming', 'Bioprofile Wash', 'Profile Spin', 'The Aquarius Wash System Plus' with 'Precision Temperature Control and Enhanced Rinse Control', 'precision water sensing' and the European Community rating of 'Class B Wash Performance and Class B Energy Efficiency'.

People are rebelling against complexity. Zanussi, in line with the emotional 1990s, has designed 'products that our consumers can fall in love with'. Their new washing machine has a name, Zoe, and is yellow with stubby legs similar to a cartoon character.

AEG's 1990 ÖKO Lavamat machines made an attempt to convince buyers that machine makers 'care' about them, especially affluent older people. 'The control panel is so logically laid out, you won't need the instruction booklet,' says the brochure. The controls are easier to read – in line with the 'age power' movement spearheaded by the Royal College of Art to abolish tiny type and controls which can't be read by our ageing population. The AEG is keen to show that it is long-lasting. A slot-in electronic control panel can be changed to update the machine without getting a new one, it uses the lowest European water (48 litres to a 5 kg wash), has a powder overdose warning light, and a halogen light so that you can see washing in the machine.

It also trumpets 'Advanced Fuzzy Logic' to decide how much water is needed per individual wash. Fuzzy logic, the buzzword of all kitchen machine makers in 1990, began as a computer term for machines which are more 'human' in their approach, which can 'forgive' an operator for not setting the controls accurately and do the desired act anyway. Fuzzy logic is used to give machines personality, claiming that, like pets, they 'learn' (remember) their user's preferences.

What of the future? The voice-activated machine will appear once the technology is perfected by computers who write from dictation. In 1953, scientists investigated a way of washing using sound waves called Vibrasonic. Five thousand vibrations a second shook the dirt out of clothes. The research stopped after deciding that it would only work when new textiles were developed.

Now some research laboratories have returned to the idea of sound-wave washing. Just as we have several different ovens in the kitchen, and CD players, mini-disks, and tape recorders, so we will also have several different kinds of washing machine, with different clothes for each.

'A gentleman should smell of nothing but fresh air.' – Beau Brummell

In the 1660s, the diarist Samuel Pepys enjoyed a naughty sight. Hanging out to dry in Whitehall was the underwear of the King's mistress, Barbara Lady Castlemaine. Wet washing could be spread on a bush or hung on a rope, fastened with wooden dolly-pegs sold by tinkers. Woollens were stretched to dry on tenterhooks, supported by tenterpoles. In Scotland, clothes were dried on tombstones to give shirts a good shape.

But in an age when a glimpse of a bare ankle was provocative, you had to be discreet. Eighteenth-century dandies like Beau Brummell were picky about where their white linen shirts were dried – not from modesty but for the right smell, sending them to Hampstead Heath or Clapham Common for that tang of ozone which is the original fabric conditioner.

The ancestor of the spin dryer is the mechanical wringer. Invented in 1859, it squeezed out water from wet washing fed through its two wooden rollers. Mangles had a different function, although they came to look like wringers. They were a kind of rotary iron, made not to wring out water but to flatten damp clothes or large linen sheets after they had been through the wringer. After that, these things would not be ironed, but might be 'pressed' by being screwed down in a sandwich between two wooden boards under a linen press.

Only the best clothes would go on to be hand-ironed. A lady's petticoat might take her maid as long as half a day. 'It was hard work; we'd all those frills and the Lord knows what,' recalled Mrs

Graham, who used flat irons at home in York. 'Old nighties were all pintucks, and oh, the christening gown, oh dear: all that embroidery anglaise work.'

The earliest mangles, invented in 1774 by Hugh Oxenham, looked like tables. Sheets or clothes were stretched over them on wooden cylinders and beaten with carved flat pieces of wood called batlets. Around 1850 came the box-mangle, a shoulder-wrenching, two-person machine. Clothes were stretched on wooden cylinders over a low wooden frame, and two of you stood at either end and used straps to push and pull a huge chest full of stones over them. Improved machines like Bradford's in 1864 added a flywheel which made the mangle move back and forth 'automatically' once it was going, and supposedly reduced this torture to a one-person job. The box-mangle led to the electric roller iron, first produced by Thor and revived in 1966 by Morphy Richards with a foot pedal control.

The box mangle died out in ordinary homes when old washing machines added two rollers above the tub which doubled as wringer and mangle. You put your clothes through and turned a handle to get the water out, then to flatten them. At first, they were turned by hand. Electricity first powered them in 1953.

The mangle could be dangerous – to fingers and other parts. Yvonne Thomas from South Wales recalls her mother's wooden mangle in the late 1940s. 'My sister Madeleine caught her long hair in it. I still remember the yells.' They could also break buttons, especially old mother-of-pearl ones. Sometimes the rollers were 'softened' with flannel wrapped around them.

Mangling, especially with cast-iron rollers, was hard on clothes. In 1865, a French inventor came up with the idea of removing water from clothes by putting them in a barrel with holes in it and spinning it very fast. Another early machine offered the option of removing the barrel of wet clothes and fixing it on a spindle at an angle, to spin off water.

Both were too far ahead of their time, but when electricity made machinery easier to power, they were remembered in 1924 by American firm Savage, which offered a washing machine that doubled as a spin dryer – not for homes but for laundries. Through the 1930s, spin dryers pop up now and again – the 1939 twin-tub, the Universal Electric Washer and Damp Dryer includes 'a dryer that needs but a minute to spin (clothes) damp-dry' and, in the same year, the Apex-Vactric 'spin and dry' doubled the spin section as a 'sterilizing rinse' tub too. But in 1956, Creda produced the first mass-market spin dryer. When Hoover's twin-tub washer/spin dryer appeared the following year, the end of the mangle was nigh. Friendly little spin dryers like the Creda Debonair (deluxe, with emptying pump) were still used until the 1970s.

Tumble Dryers

The earliest machine dryer was the Factotum, invented in 1893 by Dr Money. Really a washer-dryer, it had a gas heating element to boil the wash as it turned. Once the clothes had been wrung, they could be put back into the machine on a special wire shelf, where they were turned over the warm air from the gas heater for an hour or two.

In the 1930s, wet clothes could be dried in an electric hot-air warming cupboard or an electric heater with a wooden clothes-frame above, covered with a slip-on cover like a portable wardrobe. R. Cadisch & Sons' 1939 catalogue offered the Lanbar, an electric porcelain enamel cupboard which for a princely £14, 'dries light articles in 30 minutes; heavy in two hours'. Another defunct idea was blow-drying clothes. In 1957, Littlewoods suggests that 'every day is a fine drying day' with the Kenwood Activair. 'The only air circulator with the unique air-fresher cell into which can be inserted a cotton wool pad soaked in eau-de-cologne or favourite deodorizer.' Again, not cheap at 13 guineas.

Tumble drying was thought of in the 1930s. A film, *'Twas on a Monday Morning*, describes the communal tumble dryers of a futuristic council estate, full of happy women working in a laundry from which – the voice-over says optimistically – they have agreed to ban children. It does not say who made these dryers, but it was probably Bendix, who produced tumble dryers for the coin-op launderettes of the 1950s, and in 1957, a washing machine that could tumble dry. But the first dedicated 'tumbler dryer', as they were called, was made by Parnell in 1958. Smaller than today's tumble dryers, it was not built in, with a vent to the outside for steam to escape, but on casters to wheel around, with a grille at the back to let steam out into the room. It had four heat settings, including cold, and a 90 minute timer. Liz Jupp of Gloucestershire owns a Parnell which has been used for 40 years. 'It's noisier than modern machines,' she said. 'And it makes the room steamy. But it works well. It has a cream enamel case, a window with an opening lever, and the drum is coloured a lovely green.'

Tumbler dryers were scarce in the 1960s. They used a lot of electricity, and small kitchens didn't have room for them. By 1968, a Burco Tumblair appears at a whopping £58 10s 3d in Brian Mills catalogue, without a glass porthole. This is still such a new idea that the sales blurb spells it out: 'Take your washing out of the wringer or spin dryer, pop it into the drop-down door, dial high, medium or low heat and set the automatic timer . . . up to 6lb dry-weight clothing is safely and quickly dried with warm air, then Tumblair switches itself off.' There were objections to the noise of tumble dryers, which makers had to damp down. In 1970, John Moores Catalogue features a Tumblair with glass porthole. 'The quiet revolution in clothes drying.'

When washing machine makers like Hoover produced matching washers and tumblers, shops demanded 'stacking kits' to stand one on the other. As more women went out to work, tumble dryers allowed them to dry clothes at night. Sales were helped by fabric conditioner advertising which pitched the idea of 'softness' as a thing you should give your children if you care for them – a softness provided by clothes being tumble-dried rather than stiffened on a line. Because women at work were not there to take clothes out of the dryer, 'features' to lessen creasing from hot clothes left in a dryer for hours were added, including a cold tumble period at the end and 'intermittent' tumble which shook the clothes every half an hour. Moisture sensors, which turn off the heat when clothes are dry rather than relying on a timer, are the most worth having, said *Which?* magazine in a tumbler test of 1995. But tumble dryers will become as obsolete as mangles when the microwave dryer appears.

The Ice-Man Goeth

It is one of history's great mysteries that for centuries, inventors ignored our most obvious needs around the house. For instance, Elizabeth I used a flushing lavatory, but the rest of us had to wait another 300 years for the loo, when it was re-invented.

It was the same with the fridge. In 1748, William Cullen, a researcher at the University of Glasgow, discovered the principle that makes fridges work. In 1823, Michael Faraday also noted the phenomenon, but couldn't think how to use it. The discovery was that if you make some liquids evaporate, they absorb heat and make the air around them cooler. You can control the cold exactly by making these liquid refrigerants circulate in a closed loop, so that they evaporate and recondense.

Victorian inventors ignored the overwhelming health benefits to be gained by cooler food storage, in favour of vital aids to humankind such as the Ladies' Folding Bustle with handy built-in sewing box. So we ate more smelly, salty, saucy and stomach-churning food for years longer than necessary – not looking too closely at what was on the plate, just in case it wriggled. And then some became ill and died.

In the centuries before food was packaged with eat-by dates, people had a robust attitude to mould. They scraped it off and ate what was left. They stored day-to-day perishables on stone larder shelves, or in a meat safe, a wooden box with chicken-wire front painted blue – a colour supposed to strike fear into the hearts of hungry flies.

A lot of a housewife's time and skill was spent on preserving food when it was in season, to use it later. There were ways to keep everything. Peas, beans and pulses were dried. Meat and fish were hung inside chimneys to smoke them. Beef, mutton, cod and herring were salted or pickled in barrels. Or you might wrap something up and bury it in a hole in the ground, remembering to bang out the insects before cooking it. Eggs were pickled in jars. Fruit was bottled or made into jam. Even rose-petals could be kept to decorate cakes, by coating them with gum arabica.

The earliest canning factory was the Extensive Preservatory in Bermondsey, South London in 1812, producing tinned mutton which came to be nicknamed Sweet Fanny Adams, after a particularly gruesome murder in 1867, in which the child victim was chopped up. But far from being the sterile, safe option we know today, tinned food could add to the risks of food poisoning. If too little meat was put in to the tin, air contaminated it. One theory behind the deaths of early Arctic explorers was that they were poisoned by the lead linings of tinned food.

Tins weren't exactly fast food. Those first cans included the instructions: 'Cut round the top near to the outer edge with a chisel and hammer.' The cook could throw away her hammer and chisel in 1860, when the first tin openers appeared. They were hard work: heavy, cast-iron blades which the user had to stab into the tin and hack round it. They were often decorated in the shape of a bull's head, to match the 'bully beef' in the tins – coming from 'bouillon' or gravy which filled the tin. Even after the rotary can-opener arrived from America in the 1890s, can-opening still wasn't easy – tins were tough, especially if you forgot your opener, as Jerome K. Jerome did in *Three Men in a Boat*. In a failed attempt to open a tin, he hammered it into a shape so frightening that he threw it into the river.

There were no machines, in those days, to make ice. Ice to keep food chilled was a luxury. In a letter to her sister Cassandra in 1808, Jane Austen uses ice as the symbol of extravagance: 'for elegance and ease and luxury, I shall eat ice and drink French wine and be above vulgar economy.' From 1820, ice was cut from the Norfolk Broads and Norway and by 1830,

1,500 tons of ice was kept in a store beneath Haymarket. It was delivered to the upper classes in London by the ice-man, who came round door-to-door with his blocks of ice cradled in hay.

In 1834, an American working in London called Jacob Perkins took the Faraday discovery and used it to develop a cooling machine using water. The idea didn't reach ordinary homes. It was too sophisticated. Instead, he sold it to breweries and wholesale butchers. Then it was used to chill the holds of fast clipper ships importing ice from Norway and America. Perhaps the supply of Norfolk Broads ice had given out, or perhaps it didn't strike the right musical tinkle in drinks. For whatever reason, by 1900, we were importing over half a million tons of foreign ice, and the ice-man delivered it to all but the poorest.

At first, the household ice supply was wrapped in blankets and left in the coldest, darkest section of the larder to make it last. Eventually, special ice-boxes to hold the lumps appeared. Thomas Masters patented an 'ice-box' in 1844. Lined with a mysterious substance called 'orpholite', you topped up the ice every two days.

Ice-boxes weren't refrigerators which actively cooled food, but were closer to thermal picnic boxes, which trap cold air for as long as possible. They were pine cupboards, insulated with slate or zinc and lined with extra layers of felt and asbestos to stop the cold getting out. There were two sections: a big one for food, connected by louvres to a smaller housing at the top for the ice block. The food was cooled by the icy air drifting through the louvred dividing wall, but to be effective, the box had to be kept closed. Mrs C.S. Peel recalls in her memoirs of the 1890s, 'a refrigerator, only opened once a day, so that the kitchen people had to bethink themselves in good time of the required meat.' As the ice melted, the most efficient ice-boxes channelled the drips away and caught them in a tray underneath, which could be used to cool bottles.

Ice-boxes could be elaborate pieces of furniture. The Excelsior range of 1885, for example, included an oak-grained cupboard with two separate wine-cooling compartments and a flip-up box for changing the ice, so that you didn't have to disturb the bottles. Or you could choose a three-section pine chest, like a chest freezer. Willow's patent refrigerator of 1891 was advertised as 'a very elegant piece of cabinet furniture'. This wasn't intended for pantries, and nor would it be for long-term storage because it had a glass showcase

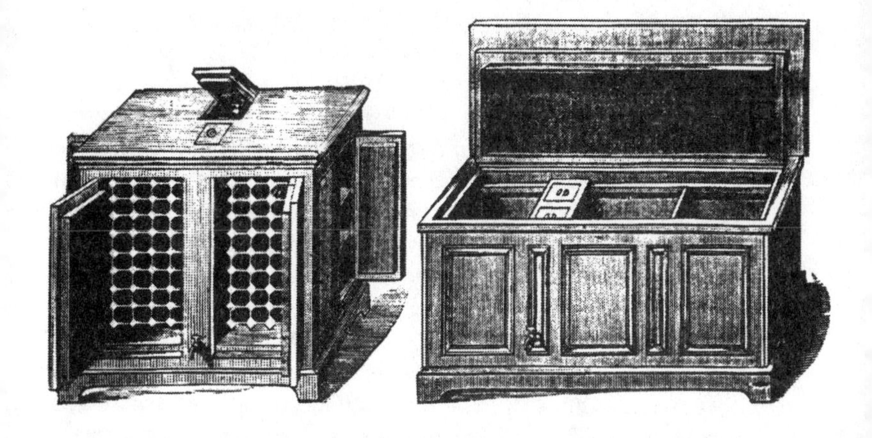

front. It could be made to match grand dining room furniture in a choice of walnut, mahogany, oak, black or gold, and tiled sides.

'Breaking the ice' at parties is a phrase which comes from those days of ice boxes and deliveries. To offer your friends drinks with ice, you had to bang bits off your big household block. Gadgets were developed to do this, like the Follows & Bate Improved Ice Breaker. It consisted of a huge hand-turned fly wheel on what looks like an office stool. You fed the ice blocks into a hopper, turned the wheel, and the crushed ice fell into a wooden drawer beneath. By the cocktail-crazy 1930s, you could buy a simpler, handier version, the Jigger Whack. A tin contained a canvas bag and a small mallet. You put the ice in the bag, then whacked it with the mallet.

Serious ice-breakers had a large heavy glass fitted with a four-footed plunger, which crushed cubes neatly. Sillier ones brandished Mr Bar Swivel, a very special telescopic bar spoon. 'Makes it easy to stir any ice drink,' runs the packaging directions. 'Hold spoon firmly at nozzle and rotate in circular motion with wrist.'

As the British colonies expanded during Queen Victoria's reign, inventors were spurred on to find new ways of mechanically cooling food so that it could be kept longer than by packing in ice or cooling with water. The farms of Australia could offer millions of tons of mutton cheaply, if only there was a way of getting it to Britain.

After a disaster in 1873 when a huge rotting cargo had to be jettisoned at sea en route from Australia, a German schoolmaster, Carl von Linde, cracked the problem by using compressed air to reduce the temperatures of insulated compartments; an idea used in America since John Gorrie developed it in 1844. In 1880, the first refrigerated mutton arrived in London from Australia. So the fridge played a vital part in establishing the economic viability of Australia, New Zealand and shortly afterwards, in developing the beef industry of South America. It also helped to establish the tradition of the Sunday roast lunch by making cheaper meat available to the masses.

We had the technology, but nobody had shrunk the refrigerator to fit a kitchen. In 1882, an American called P. Jensen tried. He came up with a 'refrigerator for domestic use' which used circulated water, but he was ahead of his time, or maybe his machine was too complicated. It wasn't until 1913 that the first electric fridge appeared, in Chicago. The Domelre (Domestic Electric Refrigerator) was followed by the Kelvinator in 1916 and Frigidaire in 1917, all from America.

These early fridges had big drawbacks. The cooling mechanism was huge. They relied on water-cooling and so had to be plumbed in to a water supply. They went wrong constantly. Tubes leaked, water pipes froze, and the compressors, thermostats and motors broke down. And they cost around $450, at a time when an average wage was less than $2000 a year. Even the rich regarded them with a puzzled eye, before concluding that they might just be useful for cooling champagne.

The fridge makers did what they could to overcome the problems. To bring down the price, they sold the cooling units separately from the food cabinets, so a family could buy the mechanism, convert their old ice box to a refrigerator and say goodbye to those daily ice-man worries.

The favourite way of doing this was to install the mechanical unit in the cellar, away from the kitchen, and connect it to the ice-box in the kitchen using pipes. So the machinery could make a noise and smell of rotten eggs (which is what sulphur dioxide does when it escapes) without giving the cook a headache. The other advantage of the split-personality fridge was that the service men, who called every three months on average, could get at the machine to oil it and check it for leaks without disturbing the family meal arrangements.

Gradually, all-in-one fridge prices dropped. In 1923, Frigidaire exported an 'electric ice box' to Britain which cost £60, the same as a second-hand car. In 1926, the price of a 10 cubic-foot fridge had crept down to £48.50. By 1932, manufacturers realised that if they made fridges smaller, they would be cheaper – though not if you look at how many cubic feet you have bought for your money. An Electrolux of 28 litres, 1 cubic foot, to take 6 pints of milk and 2 lb butter cost £19 15s 'or six pennies a week on easy terms', a sum so microscopic that it explains why early credit arrangements were called the Never-Never.

Despite all this, the ice-box stayed the norm, confusingly called 'refrigerator'. In 1921, the British Canadian Export Company advertised that their Barnet Household Refrigerator 'uses less ice than any other make', with its 11 insulating walls encased in Canadian Ash.

Fridges weren't the must-haves that they are in our era of food poisoning scares. In *First Aid to the Servantless* in 1913, Lilly Frazer discusses every topic and labour-saving appliance from dishwasher to boot-cleaner, but doesn't mention the ice-box. And in a story written in 1924, Richmal Crompton's schoolboy hero *Just William* steals left-over rice pudding from the larder shelf, not the fridge. Although his

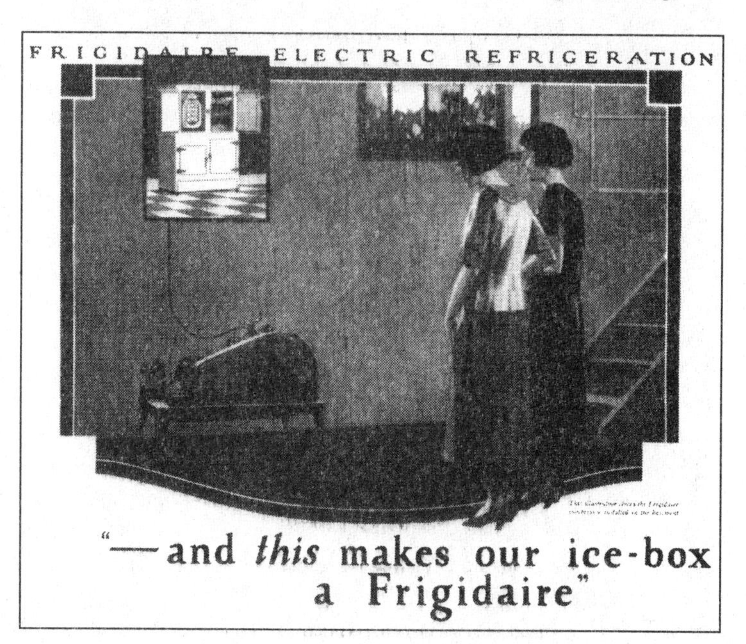

family had a cook and a maid, it seems that they didn't have an ice-box. Even in 1959, only 20 per cent of homes owned a fridge.

Why were fridges so slow to be accepted? People were suspicious, in case the early smelly refrigerants or electricity poisoned or altered the food. And a fridge would not alter life as dramatically as a washing machine. Until World War II, one could get fresh food daily without it. The streets teemed with delivery boys, their bicycle baskets stuffed with food from the butcher, baker, fishmonger and grocer. If the food was off, it was returned with complaints – as the Pooters do in *The Diary of a Nobody*, published in 1892.

In 1926, the fledgling fridge industry in Britain was given a welcome boost by an all-embracing, conveniently vague food poisoning scare in the form of The Food Preservation Act. This clamped down on a mighty list of unpleasant chemicals clandestinely and generally added to food to lengthen its shelf-life. These practices survived from before 1820, when Frederick Accum had listed them in a dramatic book with an engraving of a grinning skull over an urn wreathed in snakes and the Biblical quotation 'There is death in the pot.' His revelations included bakers pouring plaster, known as 'stuff', into bread and red lead added to anchovy sauce.

Frigidaire's advertising of the period played on the fears aroused by such 'preservatives'. It thundered: 'Most women think it is perfectly easy to detect decay in time. The truth is far different. It is there 36 hours before you can detect it. Would you let your family eat such food, mouldy food, DECAYING food?'

Fridges were also becoming more user-friendly, although this was by accident rather than by design. Faced with alternative ways of making the fridge mechanism, makers made a series of decisions which had nothing to do with the customer's convenience, and everything to do with profit. Those decisions still affect us every time our fridges emit an irritating background hum.

Fridges no longer needed to be plumbed in. Kelvinator's engineers had discovered the secret of making a closed-loop system: the characteristic fins at the back of the fridge which use air to cool it, rather than water. General Electric followed suit, and transferred its production line to making air-cooled fridges. The decision made it easier and quicker to install a fridge, and did away with frozen pipes and water leaks. The downside was that the customer paid about $3 extra a year in electricity to run it. But General Electric didn't care about that. It had a financial interest in the giant US corporation's manufacturing electricity. As General Electric's head of engineering, A.R. Stephenson, pointed out in an internal report, 'it would seem wise to exploit a machine in which the total revenue would accrue to (our) central (electricity-generating) station rather than partly to the water works.'

The second wider-reaching decision made by General Electric was to champion the compression method of cooling food. The $18 million which the company put into research and development of this method effectively stymied other kinds of fridge on the market.

For a commercial Cold War had been going on between rival makers with different cooling systems. The situation was the same as the clash between the Betamax and VHS recording methods when video appeared in the 1970s. But in the 1920s, the sparring partners were General Electric and Electrolux. Both companies used technology developed by the French. Inventing new ways of preserving food had been close to their hearts ever since Napoleon had offered a cash prize to anyone who could develop new ways of feeding his army.

The compression method, adopted by General Electric, involved a noisy motor and the stinking refrigerant sulphur dioxide.

The Swedish company Electrolux pioneered the absorption method, which relied on a gas-flame rather than a motor to control the cool temperature inside wooden refrigerators lined with cork. This technique came from an idea developed by Frenchman Ferdinand Carre in 1862. He had suggested a steam-powered version for industry, and a coal-fired version for homes. The idea was adapted for gas by two Swedish students, von Platen and Munters.

Absorption fridges had many advantages for users. They were silent, cheaper, had no mechanical parts and didn't break down. They didn't need electricity – a benefit when most ordinary people weren't connected. They could work on oil or usually gas. But they were water-cooled, so plumbing-in was essential. They used so much water that many water boards made an extra charge. The modern equivalent is a hosepipe licence. Instead of sulphur dioxide, they used ammonia, which people feared because it was toxic.

Not until 1932 did a company called Servel develop the gas fridge with an air-cooled system rather than the water one. By then, it was too late to make an impact, although the company went on making gas fridges until 1957. Electrolux fought on, and only made its first compressor fridge in 1956. As late as 1965, it claimed that absorption fridge sales were rocketing.

General Electric had started by making both compressor and absorption fridges. Among patents it had gobbled up earlier was a device developed in 1911 by a French monk, Abbé Audiffren, and it based its compression method on this. The massive sums pumped into research resulted in the Monitor Top in 1925. The earliest popular modern fridge, this was the first to have a cooling mechanism in the same unit as the food storage cupboard.

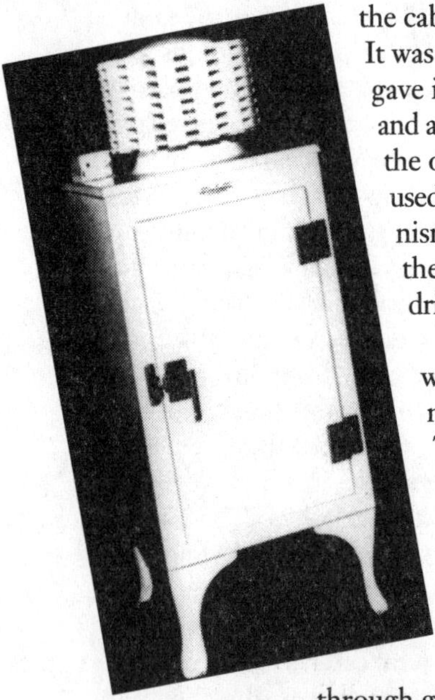

The cooling machinery was taken out of the cabinet, giving double the storage space. It was put on top, in a whorl of metal which gave it the nickname, the Beehive. Illogical and a dirt-trap, it formed a familiar link with the old ice-box designs which people were used to, which also put the cooling mechanism (the ice) on top of the machine – in their case, for the reason that cold air drifts downwards.

The beehive design looked dramatic, which was important for sales of a machine which was basically passive. There is a strong element of showmanship in selling machines, especially in an age so desperate for entertainment that a new machine would be demonstrated as part of a music-hall show. The Beehive needed a point of interest. It didn't suck up dirt through glass windows like vacuum cleaners, or spin round like washing machines. It was a huge success, selling five times more than sales forecasts of 10,000 by 1929.

Other companies joined the winners and made 'me-too' compressor fridges – the same idea, but under their label. Kelvinator spent a million dollars on research. The attractively-named Common Sense Company, by comparison, had a measly $30,000 for its gas fridge research. Gas companies didn't help the fridge makers. They tended to rest on their laurels after the success of gas lighting and cooking, hoping that the new electricity wouldn't last.

General Electric set out to capture the fridge market aggressively. It had a King Kong of a public relations department, bestriding New York by erecting a neon sign which could be read three miles away. Judson Burns, a Philadelphia fridge dealer, built his new store in the shape of the Monitor Top fridge. In 1928, a Monitor Top was sent on a submarine trip to the North Pole and this was broadcast on the popular *Believe it or not* radio programme, though it is hard to see what was said about it.

In 1929, General Electric launched its new all-steel fridge by displaying locked pirates' chests in their dealers' windows for weeks before. This 'teaser' generated such excitement that in one town, 800 people assembled to see the chests unlocked on 22 March. No one records whether their rapture when they saw that steel box pulled out matched that of General Electric's besotted executives.

The following June, bored children yanked their parents over to the fridge showroom windows to see a mechanical puppet show inside the new steel fridges.

There were three scenes. 'The Prologue: A Bride in June' showed the happy wedding in an illuminated cathedral. Then the scene revolved to 'A Servant in September', showing the unhappy housewife in a kitchen without electrical conveniences. The finale, 'Freedom in a General Electric Kitchen', revealed a modern kitchen where our heroine leapt with joy, improbably dressed in flowing white robes like the popular dancer Isadora Duncan.

This publicity battle pushed makers to new technical achievements so that they could claim that they were better than their rivals. The first 'features' in a kitchen machine, ice-making compartments, were introduced around 1925 by a Rugby-based British firm, Thomson Houston, and soon, many models were referred to in terms of how many ice cubes they would make in that tiny box at the top.

In 1930, the fridge became house-trained. The first thermostats were fitted, strips of brass and steel which bent when the fridge temperature varied and flipped switches on or off to keep a constant temperature. But the fridge really became a kitchen pet rather than a potentially smelly pest, when Frigidaire developed freons. At the time, they were what the world was looking for: artificial refrigerant liquids which weren't poisonous or flammable like ammonia and sulphur dioxide. These were chlorofluorocarbons, notorious to us as CFCs.

Freons have a story in themselves, as one of those triumphs of modern science which generate unexpected problems. This new generation of 'inert gases' were wonderful things: they were chemically highly stable, they could stand endless cooling and heating cycles, they didn't corrode the inside of the fridge, and they didn't create bad smells if they leaked. Unfortunately, because they were inert, if they leaked into the atmosphere, they didn't break down or disperse like other volatile gases, with appalling results 50 years on when they were discovered to be a cause of global warming.

But back in the 1930s, fridges had to look smart and modern if they were going to become everyday necessities. The fridges of the 1920s were designed like pieces of furniture. Electrolux's 1925 D-fridge had cabriole legs, like Chippendale, and came in dark oak. Kelvinator's K60 fridge in the 1920s came in white porcelain or futuristic silver cellulose, and heralded a complete style change, which affected the way our kitchens look right up until today.

The fashion for white enamelled steel kitchen machines arrived in the 1930s. The ultimate 30s icon is a perfectly square, gleaming white sugar lump. It was rational to use straight lines, similar to the influential German design movement, the Bauhaus. In those health-conscious times, white looked cleaner; unlike wood, it seemed to harbour no germs. Electrolux even produced a hyper-hygienic built-in fridge, for tiny kitchenettes – the first built-in kitchen machine.

Through the 1930s, top designers were hired to give a particular maker's fridge the leading edge in looks – only to be head-hunted by a rival company. Goaded by the success of the 1934 Prestcold, with ventilation fins and a foot-pedal door opener, in 1935, General Electric paid Henry Dreyfuss to turn his attention to streamlining the Monitor Top fridge. He tucked the cooling unit inside a white steel box and got rid of legs, which had made it easy for dust to gather underneath. For the new, aerodynamic shape, he was helped by technical advances in steel-making. The new fridge casings were lighter and easier to bend. But the factory could only cope with gently curved angles, accounting for the slightly flared, curve-edged look seen in the trains, planes and cars of the time.

In 1938, Hoover snitched Dreyfuss, whose design gave their fridge a look similar to the cars which were considered the last word in modernity. There were clunky car handles, outside door hinges, a badge on the front like a car badge, and inside, a light and separate boxed compartments for salads.

Among status symbols, his was a Ford in the garage; hers was a fridge in the kitchen. This was a clever marketing trick, but it wasn't plucked out of the air. The first fridges had been developed by executives in car companies as a sideline. Now car companies owned many of the big fridge makers. Frigidaire was bought by General Motors, Kelvinator, by American Motors. It was a businesslike economy of scale to double-up the same production techniques used on cars, and make similar hinges, pressings, castings and chrome plate.

There were dissenters from the streamlining craze. Creda's Electric Refrigerator looked like an art deco cocktail cabinet in oak, with circular vents on the top, which made it perfect for those whose kitchens were so small that the fridge needed to live in the lounge.

Meanwhile, the irrepressible General Electric publicity machine turned to movie-stars to give the fridge extra glamour. *Three Women* was an hour-long film starring Hedda Hopper. The publicity handout was characteristically modest. 'It is the most pretentious, the most beautiful, the most effective commercial story ever told on the talking screen,' it trilled. 'For glorious colour and amazing realism, it is on a par with outstanding examples of cinema artistry.' The plot? 'An

interesting story in which comedy and romance are skilfully blended, all of which pivots and revolves around the complete electric kitchen.'

In an attempt to make the fridge the hip accessory for the young bride, General Electric also produced an HMV-label fridge. It was as if Virgin Records suddenly produced fridges today. 'The HMV electric refrigerator is made to the same high standard as "His Master's Voice" radio, records and gramophones,' runs the advertisement, adding thoughtfully to its music-loving audience, 'will not interfere with your radio.' This sounds like an absorption fridge. 'The HMV is the only refrigerator fitted with the unique Silent Circulator cooling mechanism, which never wears out, needs little attention, runs at negligible cost.'

The gas fridge was slower to die out in Britain. In 1936, the Good Housekeeping Institute had recommended a gas Electrolux fridge ('the flame that freezes') for its Ideal Kitchen, and the fridges were installed at Windsor Castle. But in September 1937, the magazine turned to electric compressor fridges, recommending a fridge which seems incredibly complex. The Apex-Vactric had 'all modern innovations', which were: quietness, a light inside, with an illuminated control-dial; removable shelves; ice-creating storage tray and a baffling choice of 15 freezing speeds.

Having done everything they could to a fridge's outside, the designers moved to its inside. In 1935, Walter Dorw came up with the first fridge with storage in the door – Crosley's Shelvador. At the same time, Raymond Loewy designed the Coldspot Refrigerator for Sears Roebuck, the American mail order firm. Advertised as 6 cubic feet for half the usual price, a very conservative $250, this 'study in beauty' boasted four storage baskets and a water cooler. A year later, it was advertised in Britain by Berry Brothers on polar theme, all the rage after crowds flocked to admire the modernist Penguin Pool at London Zoo: 'The puffin, as a Northern creature, appreciates each Coldspot feature.'

World War II took the fridge factories away to making weapons, and afterwards, they turned to export drives to make up their shattered fortunes.

The majority went fridge-less, though they aspired to having a fridge. But if you wanted to wow your friends, you could buy a pretend one: a white steel 'food cabinet' at £4 3s, from Littlewoods, 1948.

Previously, only the well-off had fridges. Now the very poor, ironically, had first access to the new fridges. This was the period

when the poor were guinea-pigs for futuristic machines and social experiments. They couldn't complain. Electrolux supplied the Government with thousands of fridges to be built in to prefabs, the bungalows hastily constructed for bombed-out, homeless families.

By 1951, people wanted colour to match a new air of optimism. That was the year of the first fashion fridge. The French Frimatic had a new tall, boxy look. The door opened full length because the cooling mechanism was tucked out of sight, behind the food storage area. Considered slimline, it would seem chunky to us, and its spaces for bottles and eggs seem miniscule. It used the latest advances in plastic-making to offer a salmon pink interior. Doors were coloured green, ivory, red, yellow or even black. 'We did post office red on the shop floor,' recalls Jim Smart, who sold them at John Lewis. 'But they weren't successful and we flogged them off in the end.'

In 1953, the budget cut taxes, and there was a spending boom on labour-saving machines, including fridges. The House of Lords debated whether the Warrington Electricity Showroom was blasphemous in showing a Christmas window display of wise men's gifts – a trio of fridge, washing machine and cooker. Fridges became sexy for a time, after Marilyn Monroe revealed that this was where she kept her jeans.

American films showed huge fridges, where all-providing Momma kept apple pie. Britain's new semi-detached houses had tiny narrow kitchens and if you had a fridge, it was small. Prestcold produced a wall-hung fridge. Others tried to make disguisable fridges. The Coldette of 1955 was housed in a wooden cabinet so that it could go in the sitting room.

In 1954, food rationing ended. We had access to more food than ever. To hold it, those American larder fridges like Kelvinator's Fooderama reached Britain. New house builders cut costs by leaving out the walk-in larder, forcing people to invest in a fridge, and a kitchen cupboard with a drop-down flap. 'It's love at first sight for this new COLDRATOR,' croons an ad in *Good Housekeeping* in 1957. 'New! Door shelves. New! Coloured table tops . . . and if you had X-ray eyes, you'd be even more impressed.' And again, 'News for houseproud housewives! New! Own a genuine Frigidaire for only 15 guineas in Cotswold Cream, Sherwood Green, Mayfair Pink, Olympic Red or Ivory White.'

People looked – and then settled for cheaper, bland, white fridges. During the 1960s and 70s, the fridge sat in the corner, humming to itself and going nowhere. Fridges went from must-haves to has-beens. An influx of cheap, continental brands like Indesit appeared, putting old fridge makers like Prestcold and English Electric out of business.

To move the stagnant market, makers added 'features' – gimmicks. Hotpoint copied the American idea of putting a drinks dispenser tap in the door. People were fascinated by it and rationalized their desire to buy it by telling themselves that it would encourage their children to drink more orange juice, but ultimately, it created an extra chore: to fill the fridge door and check that the juice was still fresh.

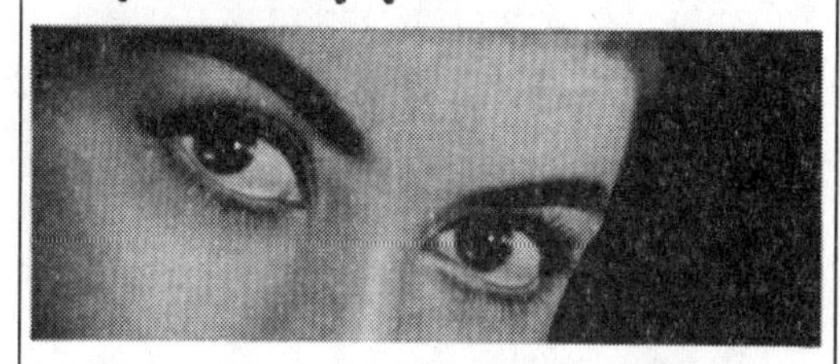

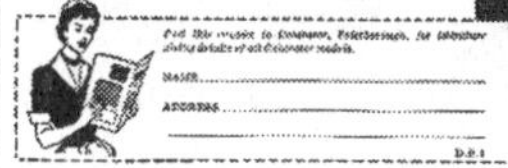

Push-button defrosting arrived in 1959, so that women did not have the chore of turning the fridge off, hacking at the ice with a plastic trowel thoughtfully provided by the makers, then letting the remains slowly drip out to spoil the new kitchen lino. In the 1970s, women wanted anything time-saving, and feminist feeling focused on the kitchen. A revolutionary, casual attitude to food and housework was summed up by Shirley Conran's famous phrase, in her book *Superwoman*: 'Life is too short to stuff a mushroom.'

What could fridges offer the New Woman? Not much more than self-defrosting. Even that presented problems. The system worked by trickling melted ice down the back of the food storage area, where it made its way through a small hole to a metal cup on the hot part of the motor at the back, to evaporate. But the holes became blocked by crumbs. Storing food in a clinical, Clingfilm wrapping was the same. People stored food loose. Crumbs and vegetable leaves made the fridges break down. Jim Smart of John Lewis recalls a highly technical way of sorting this out. 'Our engineers cleared the blockages with a knitting needle.'

The feminists of the 1970s were having families and kitchens became larger, and important as the centres of home life in the 1980s. Built-in units, an American idea which made kitchens easier to clean, appeared. To match them, Continental companies AEG, Miele and Bosch made the first built-in fridges, which could be hidden behind doors.

Perhaps fridges were hidden like this because food became an embarrassing subject. People ate less. Diana, Princess of Wales became the most famous anorexic, summing up a Jekyll and Hyde attitude to food: we had more choice than ever, but felt we should eat less. Nouvelle cuisine extolled its doll's-house size vegetables.

There were exceptions. At the opening of London's Design Museum in 1989, crowds surged admiringly around Zanussi's Wizard fridge, designed by Roberto Pezzatta. Conceived as a piece of post-modernist art in the tradition of Memphis, the Italian design house considered the apotheosis of cool, this had an £850 steel casing in grey or black to match the clothes of yuppies who, it was hoped, would buy it. It was intended to be beautiful all round, to stand in one of the latest open-plan warehouse flats.

The Wizard broke the tradition of the fridge as a rectangular metal box by being topped with a frivolous pointed metal hat flying a red metal flag, like a sandcastle. But it hardly reached shops, because the door at the back left nowhere for the heat to get out, and the result was constant breakdown.

Fridges became even more unpopular as the 1980s wore on. They were seen as electricity guzzlers. New laws obliged shops to rate all new fridges for energy-consumption. Electrolux, which now owned many other fridge companies including Zanussi, AEG, Kelvinator, Frigidaire and White Westinghouse, was the first to make a Low-Energy Refrigerator. That halved electricity consumption, it claimed, to less than that used by a 20-watt lightbulb.

Even worse was the problem caused by CFCs and their variant, HFCs. The miracle refrigerant liquids of the 1930s were highlighted in the 1980s as one of the principal culprits behind global warming. The gases they emit attack the ozone layer, which protects the growth of ocean phytoplankton. In 1990, 170 international scientists issued a stark warning in a report by the Intergovernmental Panel on Climate Change, that unless we took immediate action, temperatures would rise, causing the greenhouse effect which would fatally affect Earth's environmental balance. The early 1990s saw most Western countries agreeing to phase out CFCs. Fridge makers had to find alternative refrigerants. Electrolux took the lead, with its subsidiary AEG launching CFC-free fridges in 1993.

People went back to nature. 'Many families are finding that the larder solves most of their cold storage problems,' warned *Traditional Kitchens* magazine. 'The standard internal temperature of most refrigerators is 4 degrees centigrade – too cold for many cooling purposes – and in such circumstances wine can lose its bouquet, beer its head and vegetables some of their taste . . . you may find that a smaller capacity fridge is adequate.'

Philips launched a Food Conservation Centre at a thousand pounds. The idea was a flexible larder-cum-fridge. Three separate cold zone compartments could be adjusted at the flick of a switch, giving more freezing space for garden harvests, or 'cellar' cold for Christmas drinks. The idea appealed to the middle classes with a new interest in French cheeses and wine, to be kept without the flavour being frozen out of them.

In the 1990s, food has become entertainment. Fridges have come out of hiding to be centrepieces for the kitchen. Zanussi and Bosch have produced huge, 1930s-reminiscent fridges in bright blue, red and yellow. Atag's eye-catching circular designs were cited by *T5* magazine as one of the top most desirable machines in the world at £3145.

Fridges have become huge to hold the growing number of chilled, ready-cooked meals which are bought by women who don't shop as frequently as their mothers did, because they work or have other priorities. Chilled meals from the fridge are no longer considered second-best. It may be that the standards of ready-cooked chilled meals are so high that they undermine women's confidence in their own abilities to do better – an interesting result of refrigeration.

The earliest fridges were sold on an advertising platform of playing on our anxieties about food poisoning. If anything, despite widespread refrigeration, our worries about food have become worse. Listeria and e-coli will play their part in developing the fridges of the future. So-called 'smart' technology – electronics incorporated into 'thinking' pro-active machines which do our work before we have even thought of it – has suggested the food poisoning alert fridge. Belgian designer Bart Nelid, from the firm Living Tomorrow, described his idea in the *Daily Mail* in 1998. 'Food is scanned as it is placed inside the fridge so its computer can keep track of what is being used. It's also possible to devise a programme to flash a warning when the sell-by date is passed.' Another idea comes from Germany: a fridge which stores a databank of a thousand recipes and can suggest a meal, by comparing the recipes with the food it contains at that moment.

The Big Freeze

In 1626, the Elizabethan philosopher Francis Bacon became the first martyr to kitchen appliances. He died of pneumonia after stuffing snow into freshly killed chickens to freeze them, hoping to make them last longer.

The idea of ice as a food preserving method is as old as the mountains. The Romans collected ice from the Alps and moved it in straw-covered wagons to ice cellars in Rome to keep food cool for their fantastic banquets of fish and shellfish. They imported oysters to Britain from Northern France and Spain to as far inland as St Albans, and kept them in holes surrounded by ice, insulated with straw.

The idea of freezing was re-introduced from the Continent by returning Royalists. In 1666, a 'snow-well' was sunk in St James's Palace for the Duke of York. This was a thatched hole lined with ice chunks, probably from one of the cleaner stretches of the River Thames. Ice was exclusive. A few years later, Samuel Pepys was thrilled to be offered wine with ice in it.

BY ROYAL LETTERS PATENT.

MARSHALL'S PATENT FREEZER.

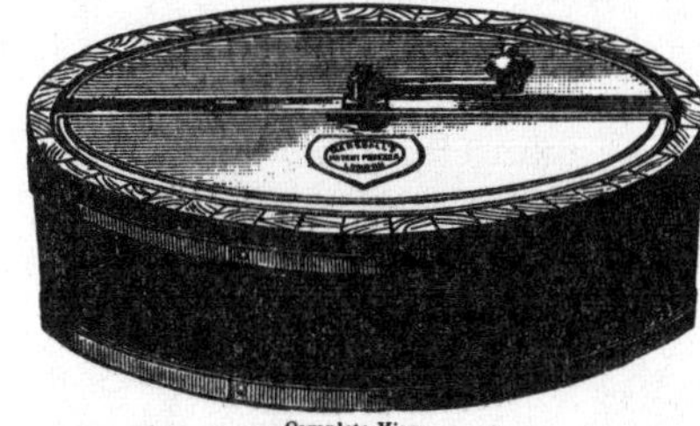

Complete View.

IS PRAISED BY ALL WHO KNOW IT FOR

CHEAPNESS in first cost. CLEANLINESS in working.
ECONOMY in use. SIMPLICITY in construction.
RAPIDITY in Freezing.

NO PACKING NECESSARY. NO SPATULA NECESSARY.

Smooth and delicious Ice produced in 3 minutes.

SIZES—No. 1, to freeze any quantity up to one qt., £1 5 0. No. 2, for two qts., £1 15 0. No. 3, for four qts., £3 0 0. No. 4, for six qts., £4 0 0. Larger sizes to order.

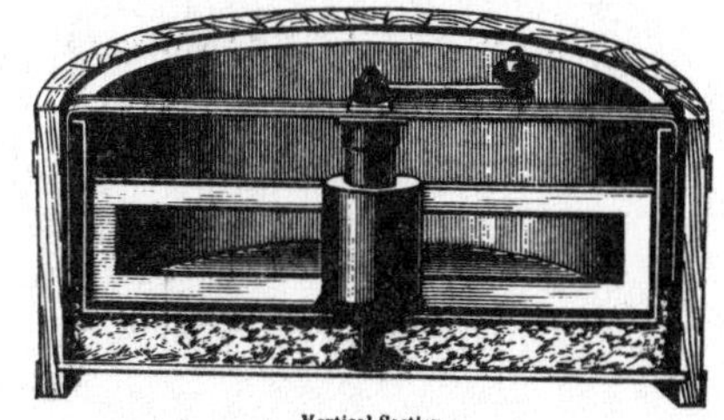

Vertical Section.

Showing the fan inside, which remains still while the pan revolves and scrapes up the film of ice as it forms on the bottom of the pan. The ice and salt is also shown *under* the pan; there is no need to pack any round the sides.

Frozen desserts found their way on to eighteenth-century menus, helped by the influx of French cooks escaping from the Revolution, who brought a new sophistication to British tables. By the 1800s, all aristocratic homes had an ice house and ices had become a craze. The most fanciful were disguised as follies or pagodas, but a typical ice house was built like a brick igloo, twenty feet deep into the sides of the gloomiest, coldest area of the grounds, reached through a curved passage which stopped warm air blowing in, and with two front doors, two walls and a two-foot layer of reeds plastered on the outside to keep the cold in.

Ice for the ice house was grown on special ice ponds next to it. We imagine that people had a sketchy idea of the importance of food hygiene in the past. But the method of gathering ice at Chatsworth in Derbyshire shows that people went to considerable pains to keep it clean. At first nip of frost, a groundsman would flood the pond with fresh water, swooshing away the leaves which had collected. Then a gamekeeper stood guard round the clock to scare away birds and animals until the ice was an inch thick.

It was harvested by a six-man team, recalls Dennis Fischer, who spent his youth as a 'fetcher', bringing rum and beer to warm the men during the day. 'Men's boots (there were no Wellingtons in those days) and all tools were kept scrupulously clean, and care had to be taken not to stir up the water when breaking the ice,' he said. 'The slightest particle of mud, leaf, bird dropping or even blade of grass contaminated the ice; nor was it ever stored if covered, even only slightly, with snow, as apparently this melted and prevented the complete solidification of the ice.'

Standing on the edges, the men would cut the central area of the pond and break it into smaller chunks with special mallets. Then they pushed it through a wooden chute into the underground ice house. Here it would sit, slowly melting. Woe betide the man who was sent to get the ice during the year. He would often slip, especially if he had to climb a ladder to chip off a chunk at the top. Ice house accidents formed sensational stories in newspapers.

In his book, *Cottage Economy*, written in 1821, do-gooder William Cobbett suggested that 'the labouring classes' might like to build their own ice house. He asserts that underground ice houses are useless because they are too damp, so suggests that the labourer builds his ice house 'quite open to the sun and air'. A pretty thatched building would be appropriate in his opinion. He admits that he has never tried his plan out, adding, 'If the thing fail as an ice house, it will serve generations to come as a model for a pig bed.'

Cooks could make ice cream years before we could make ice itself, in complicated copper shapes or moulds without the aid of a machine. The cook would mix cream by the quart with fruit purée and egg yolks, then hand-stir the mixture for two hours over a wooden pail filled with ice, mixed with salt to stop it melting.

Ice creams were showily presented. An apricot-flavoured ice cream would be moulded as an apricot, painted with food colour, with the apricot stalk and leaves added. An Edwardian illustration shows ices in the shapes of bunches of grapes, pomegranates, with seeds, and even roses and lilies with petals.

To the Victorians, ice was fascinating and exotic. One of Sherlock Holmes' most famous cases tells how the victim was stabbed to death

in a Turkish bath – with a knife fashioned from ice, which melted, leaving no incriminating evidence. Sorbets – iced sugar, water and flavouring – were particular favourites. Queen Victoria routinely served twelve courses at lunch and dinner, and after the sixth course, a sorbet flavoured with port, brandy or rum. It was supposed to aid digestion.

The closest the Victorians got to a freezer were ice-cream freezing machines. These were invented far earlier than refrigerators, cutting the time taken to freeze the ice from two hours to 20 minutes. The first was patented in 1843 by Nancy Johnson.

These manual ice-cream making machines, like the Frezo, Star and Paragon, cost as much as £5, but were considered genteel accessories for middle-class homes. They were called 'crank' freezers because to use them, you cranked a handle. There was an outer wooden pail for the ice which provided the freezing. Inside this sat a tin or pewter cylinder. Here you poured the ice cream mixture, then bolted down the lid and turned the handle sticking through the top, which stirred a device inside called the dasher. Some models had a divided inner bucket, so that you could make two flavours at once, presumably with two stirrers so that they did not mix together. A different design was patented by Agnes Marshall. This had shallow sides and reduced freezing time to three minutes. Agnes experimented with making ice with liquefied gas in 1901, suggesting that

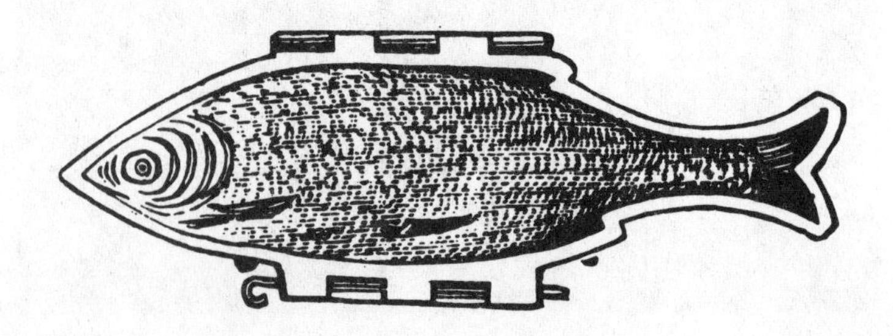

servants could hand it round at dinner tables so that guests could make instant personalised ice creams.

Until the 1930s, people were happy to spend large sums on home ice-cream making machines, when few of them bothered to buy an ice-box for staples, like butter and milk. Maud Lancaster, writing *A Manual of Electricity in the Service of the Home* as 'Housewife' in 1914, sheds some light on the attitudes that shaped this preference. 'In England the weather is seldom hot enough for many days together, to justify, in the opinion of most housewives, the expense of a refrigerating outfit,' she opines. 'A small ice-making plant can be bought for a few pounds and will prove extremely useful, while in the smaller households a freezing machine, electrically driven, will save much work when ice cream is required during the summer.'

BY ROYAL LETTERS PATENT.

MARSHALL'S PATENT ICE CAVE.

Charged ready for use.

USES.

FOR SETTING ICE PUDDINGS without the use of grease or chance of brine entering, and without the expense of special moulds. Ice puddings when moulded can be turned out and kept ready for use at any minute, so that the ice can be made and held ready before commencing to serve the dinner if necessary.

FOR FREEZING SOUFFLÉS it offers great advantages, as the progress of freezing can be examined from time to time. The soufflés can always be kept ready for use.

FOR INVALIDS to have always at hand a supply of ice or iced food or drink, or for food or drink to be kept hot for any length of time. It is especially useful in nurseries, in the latter respect.

FOR CONFECTIONERS to send out ice puddings, etc., quite ready for serving; for keeping ice creams, etc., ready for selling.

FOR KEEPING ICES during Balls, Evening and Garden Parties, and for taking ice creams, etc., to Races, Picnics, etc.

AND FOR REFRIGERATORS GENERALLY.

SIZE No. 1 will hold one quart mould. Size 2, two quart moulds. Size 3, four quart moulds. Size 4 will hold six large champagne bottles. Sizes No. 2 and upwards can be used for icing mineral waters, etc., and kept in dining, smoking, and billiard rooms.

PRICES.

No. 1, £1 11*s*. 6*d*. No. 2, £2 2*s*. No. 3, £3 3*s*. No. 4, £4 4*s*. Larger and special sizes to order.

She has a freezing machine in mind: the Federal Domestic, a huge electric engine connected to a fly wheel which stirs a tiny bucket containing three quarts of ice cream. The cost is under 1d an hour, though 'it is seldom wanted for more than half an hour at a time.'

There were other powered ice machines. The most popular was most like a compressor fridge, a machine which used a piston to compress air and produce cold, developed by H.C. Ash in 1860. This was considerably easier to work than other machines, and over 25 years later, Mrs Beeton's *Household Management* recommended it as 'a pleasant and easy amusement for ladies.'

Most people stuck to small, hand-turned freezers. Their names melt on the tongue. The Champion Ice-Making Machine, the Reliance Freezer, the White Montana Freezer and the Lightning (63 shillings from Gamages in 1908).

An advertisement from the Cincinatti Gooch Freezer Company of 1889 is disarmingly honest. 'The PEERLESS are the best. But they are a little higher priced than others, but are well worth the difference. The ZERO is cheaper, not so good as the PEERLESS, but better than any other freezer on the market. The PET, cheaper than the ZERO, and a very good one. The Boss is very low priced. Anybody could afford to buy one. All are good, solid and well-made.'

MAKE YOUR OWN ICE-CREAM

Without Trouble, Turning or Mess

A NEW IDEA IN ICE-CREAM FREEZERS

Vacuum Process

With the Iceberg Ice-Cream Freezer all you have to do to make *Delicious, Luscious, Refreshing, Appetising Ice-Cream* is to pack the Freezing Compartment with Ice and Freezing Salt, close it down, and then fill the Central Chamber with the Creaming Mixture. In half an hour you have Ice-Cream fit to place before the best in the Land, including yourself, your family and your guests.

The tiresome task of more or less continuous turning a handle is entirely done away with.

YOU SIMPLY FILL—IT DOES THE REST

The "Iceberg" Rapid Freezer is made in three sizes to suit all requirements.

Size 1.	1 Imperial Quart	21/-	Post Free
Size 2.	2 American Quarts	27/6	,, ,,
Size 3.	4 ,, ,, ...	52/6	,, ,,

AS SHOWN AT THE "IDEAL HOME EXHIBITION" WHERE THOUSANDS WERE SOLD

Send for an "Iceberg" Freezer to-day, and be prepared for one of the greatest pleasures of a Hot Summer's Day. Ideal for Picnics by Motor or by Boat.

COMMERCIAL MONOPOLIES LTD. (Dept. 90), 56 Ludgate Hill, E.C.4

Vacuum ice-cream makers like Gamages' Beldray Rapid appeared at the turn of the century, and made ice cream in two shakes, literally. 'The vacuum freezer is very handy for picnics or boating excursions as it is easily carried and the freezing can be done en route,' explains *Good Housekeeping* in fun-loving 1922, adding that with no moving parts, there was 'nothing to be got out of order'.

The vacuum ice-maker consisted of

two enamelled tinplate cylinders which slid together. You packed the outer cylinder with the ice and coarse freezing salt, or the new labour-saving 'inexhaustible freezing crystals' from America. The inner chamber held the fruit and cream purée. You sealed it, turned it upside down once or twice, then stirred it occasionally during the next 20 minutes.

The new electricity industry produced small ice-cream makers in the 1920s and 30s, as add-on accessories to food mixers, like one from the Troy Metal Products Company of 1922. Plugged into a light socket, it was a large motor attached to the top of a hood holding, among other things, a colander, coffee grinder and vegetable cutter. These weren't cheap. In 1931, a mixer with a freezing attachment cost £24.

Freezing turned from a lady's party-trick into a serious method of preserving everyday food when American inventor Clarence Birdseye went on a hunting trip to Labrador in 1923. He noticed that the eskimos left reindeer and fish packed in ice at remote points, returning months later to collect and cook them. Back in America, he adapted their technique by fast-freezing food between metal plates, and patented the process in 1925. His first frozen food was sold in 1928.

Birdseye did not expect people to buy his frozen food to store at home. Frozen peas, his first line, were sold from the shop freezer to be eaten next day at home. But in New York, food could be stored in short-term freezers. Smart apartment blocks supplied each occupant with an 'ice locker' just as they had a box for post.

Electrolux brought out the first air-cooled freezer, CH2, in 1938, but during the war, the factories were turned over to munitions. Birds Eye frozen peas reached Britain in 1946, and in 1948, *Vogue* commented that 'The new look has spread to the larder, insomuch that 'quick freeze' methods have come to stay, turning our bill of winter fare topsy turvy.' There was a general air of approval: it pointed out that freezing could eliminate wasted food and save time.

All the same, home freezers didn't appear in Britain until 1951. Their maker, the American Deep Freezer Company, gave us the phrase 'deep freezing' but ironically, it took another four years to develop the technology allowing freezers to reach the -18 degrees centigrade needed to freeze food.

Gradually, frozen food appeared in the shops. At first, they sold packets of vegetables. Birds Eye fish fingers, in 1955, were a very new idea. They changed our eating tastes and heralded the beginning of a new industry in frozen, breadcrumbed meat and fish shapes for children.

In 1956, Electrolux produced the first chest freezer. The City Box looked like a washing machine, with a small top through which you rummaged for the food. Presumably the name was chosen to suggest trendiness, but when *Good Housekeeping* enthusiastically took up the idea the following year, it suggested that freezers were good for people who lived in the country.

Fridges had had a tiny ice-cube tray at the top since the 1920s. The fridge-freezer was born when fridges offered a small frozen food section in 1959. This began as no more than a box for a block of Wall's Ice Cream, but grew to the full width of the top of the fridge until in 1962, English Electric took this to a logical conclusion by bringing out the Fresh 'n' Freeze fridge-freezer. Although the early fridge-freezers shared a compressor, this made the freezer part less effective at low room temperatures, for a higher cost than two separate machines. Even in 1980, the Brian Mills mail order catalogue offered only one fridge-freezer, a Zanussi which would have been among the lower priced, but cost a whopping £319.99.

There was a lot of confusion about how long frozen food could last, and the fridge industry agreed on a three-star system. One star on the freezing section meant that food could be stored for a week; two stars, a month; three stars, three months.

Front opening freezers were first seen in 1961, when as a solution for a small flat, a matching side by side fridge and freezer were built in to its kitchen. But the freezers which really took off were the cavernous chest designs of the 1970s. Says Jim Smart, of John Lewis: 'People went mad on buying them, so much so that John Lewis brought out our own brand, in three sizes. People bought meat in bulk – half a lamb from the butchers, cut into cooking packs. But that craze waned because they only ate the best joints, and were left with the others. Eventually they had to give them away.'

Freezing developed a suspect, second-best image from those early years, because people didn't understand how to freeze. Restaurants served food which was undefrosted in the middle. Shops sold unwrapped berries and vegetables straight from the freezer. Freezing was expected to miraculously make poor quality food more palatable, or turn back the clock on food which had been putrifying the day before.

The first ready-prepared meals came from Birds Eye in 1960, and were made for hospitals. In April 1972, Marks & Spencer introduced frozen meals, and a new culture was born – that of extremely high quality frozen meals which could be defrosted and eaten after work. 'The St Michael range differs from most other well-known brands of frozen foods,' says its staff newsletter. 'It concentrates on high quality dishes like lasagne and pizza which can be heated and served within minutes – speciality recipes which normally only the most ambitious cook with plenty of time would attempt to prepare.' Among the best-sellers were fisherman's pie and savoury pancakes.

It was in shops' interests to install freezers and encourage food makers to come up with delicious frozen food. This new 'convenience food' need not be sold within a day or so of arriving on the shelf. It could sit around for longer without going off, and therefore the shop would make more money.

For families, the freezer, and frozen food, changed what came to be called their lifestyle. It made an extraordinary change to women's independence and equality just when they wanted it, in the 1970s. Women were less tied to the kitchen – and had more time to work – because with a freezer, they could shop once a week, or less, to feed their family, rather than having to spend time every day buying perishable food. The result has been the growth of supermarkets. Food shops became bigger and the one-stop shop, with everything under the same roof, was born. Men tended to share the 'big shop', the main Saturday shopping, to help carry the increased loads of food. So as shopping became less a female, solitary trip, and more a communal, family occupation, sex barriers were broken down.

These changes happened gradually. In 1980, the Brian Mills mail order catalogue displayed an LEC chest freezer at £127.99 or a larger upright Electrolux at £175. But it felt the need to explain and educate would-be buyers. 'Freeze your food bills . . . enjoy the convenience of fresh food always to hand,' it said. This was a puzzling one. Frozen food could never be fresh, by definition. And people justified buying the fashionable new freezers on the grounds of thrift, only to find stocking up with food involved huge outlay. The food was not cheaper than fresh food because there were processing and packaging costs to be paid for, and particularly items like frozen prawns were realized to be bad bargains because each one had to be coated expensively in ice. Freezer-owners also had extra expenses, like special freezer bags, labels, waterproof markers, aluminium boxes and freezer film for storing your own cooked food.

Newspaper stories about people losing food worth hundreds of pounds through freezer breakdowns had proved a powerful deterrent to buyers, and as a result of the new technology, insurance companies had to offer a new kind of insurance against this happening.

Freezer technology improved in line with refrigeration generally. Philips introduced frost-free freezing in 1980, which meant that freezers never had to be defrosted. Freezers now come with temperature alarms and the self-shutting doors to guard against accidentally leaving them open.

In the 1980s, frozen food became less popular as people demanded healthy, fresh and seemingly more interesting food from the chiller cabinet instead. The ice cream industry, always central to freezing, unexpectedly rescued that image. Häagen-Dazs, an American ice cream, boldly charged huge sums and advertised using fashion pictures of couples, which made frozen food seem sexy and adult. Once again, ice cream was as desirable as it was in the 1800s. In 1998, superchef Gary Rhodes launched his own range of frozen meals which aim to replicate his restaurant dishes.

Despite all this, the 1990s has an uneasy, double view of the freezer. It is a necessary tool, but not a health aid, and the ecological campaigners have yet to really get their teeth into the implications of freezer packaging, with its huge reliance on aluminium foil and plastics.

Food That Smells of Gas and Tastes of Electricity

LOOK at the illustrations in nursery rhymes. You'll get a good idea of the way we cooked from the Norman invasion until 150 years ago. The boiling cauldron hooked up the chimney so conveniently for catching wolves, and the meat roasting on a spit turned by a little dog in front of the fire look primitive. In fact, the food they produced was more ambitious than today's superchef creations.

Out of his fireplace, a medieval high-class cook would regularly produce banquets with 20 or more hot dishes on the table at once, like spiced turbot, peacocks with edible gilding, roast cranes, tiny larks' tongues in piquant sauce, porpoise flavoured with mustard and roasted whale with peas. Not to mention soups coloured in stripes with orange saffron. The crowning glory of a meal was a 'soltelte', a sweet 'subtlety' filled with 'blamange' or jelly, decorated with painted pictures of hunting scenes, ships or even a church interior with all its altars. It was made to be eaten. By the time the kitchen had also conjured up snacks like 'towres' of giant fried eggs with several yolks in the middle, it was no wonder that Henry VIII sported a 54-inch waist.

A cook needed strong arms and fireproof hands in those days in order to co-ordinate all the gadgets used to cook a meal over an open fire, in a cauldron hung by a chain, hooked on to a horizontal beam in the chimney. To control the pot's cooking temperature, he or she reached over the fire to heave the cauldron up and down over the flames, as it hung on a 'pot hook', which had a series of notches for the pot handle.

Everyday meals were cooked in one pot. Even an easy dish, like a 'potage' (soup) of cabouches (cabbages) served to Richard II, needed attention. The cook had to check that soot hadn't got into it, and to make sure that an overboiling pot had not 'pist out the fire', as the *Ladies Dictionary* of 1694 delicately put it. A bigger meal would include meat, dumplings, vegetables and pudding, all boiled in one pot, in the same water, but in separate nets, with faster-cooking foods added later so that all the foods were ready at the same time. Who cared if a sweet pudding might carry a suggestion of boiled rabbit? It was this one-pot way of cooking which made us a nation of expert pudding cooks.

Cooking took time and money. In those fridge-less times, it tended to start with finding fresh food, hence recipes began 'first catch your chicken'. So in towns, people bought takeaways from sellers with trays round their necks, like simple Simon the pieman. They also ate out a lot at cookshops: the poor because they didn't have the equipment, fuel or time to cook; and the rich, to meet their friends, play cards and flirt with waitresses, and the food was as good as at home. You could stand around fried fish stalls like those at London Bridge, where the fish was hauled in from the Thames. William FitzStephen advised weary travellers who had just hit town to go down to the waterside 'where all things desirable are ready to their hand' in his *Description of London* in 1174.

By Tudor times, cooking equipment had become more sophisticated, partly because skilled Protestant German ironworkers had emigrated to Britain to evade religious persecution. With their input, cooking wasn't a sleeve-scalding job anymore. Cooks didn't have to reach the pot over the fire. Instead, it was hung from a chimney crane – an iron post fixed to the floor at the side of the fireplace which one could swing over the fire or away from it. A baking oven might be built into the side of the fireplace, next to a small niche for salt and another for gunpowder, both kept dry by the heat.

This was Merrie England, and travellers flocked from Europe to sample our roast beef. Actually, we preferred venison. Among the hunting-mad toffs, it was the snob animal to kill. The richer they were, the more they hunted. The more they killed, the more they ate. They feasted on so much meat that from the evidence of their medical records, Henry VIII, Mary I, Elizabeth I and Cardinal Wolsey may have suffered from scurvy, an illness caused by lack of fresh fruit and vegetables. To roast meat, they skewered it on a hand-turned spit in front of the fire. There might be two or three spits going at the same time, resting on spit-dogs at each side of the fire, which were not animals but iron holders. If you were cooking for a party, a hearth might take six or seven spits on a cabiron – a stand which was angled away from the fire at 60 degrees.

Food historian Ivan Day is an expert Tudor cook. He teaches authentic old English cookery using antique equipment in his kitchen. 'Spits were massive, often 1 inch thick, and 6 feet long,' he explains. 'If you put a small pig on them, they bend like a skipping rope, so they had to be sturdy.' They were also flat in the middle for 3 feet or so to hold the animal body firmly, otherwise it would slide around the spit as it turned and only one side would get cooked.

'There's a lot of mythology about the food having a charcoal taste,' Ivan says. 'It didn't. Everyone imagines that Elizabethan kitchens had a lovely cooking smell, but because of the intense heat, the draught gets drawn up the chimney and you can't smell anything while you're cooking. You only smell it when you put it on a platter.'

Spit cookery was faster than modern roasting. A piece of lamb weighing 11 lb might take an hour and a half. That cliché of every film, the roast ox on the banquet table, was a bit of a joke even in Tudor times. Oxen were never cooked whole on spits, except as a party-piece outdoors. They would usually take a small pig. The head and tail ends, at the far end of the flames, cooked more slowly than the body. To cook the meat evenly, the body was shielded from the flames with a rectangular shield or pig-iron hooked to the middle of the grate. It was taken down when the top and tail were a little better done.

Turning the spit was uncomfortably hot for the turnspits or skip-jacks, usually small boys. So they were protected from the fire by straw archery targets soaked in water. From the sixteenth century on, a breed of small dogs called 'turncurs' took over – if you could catch them and fasten them inside a wheel in a cage. They 'used to hide themselves or run away when they observed indications that there was to be a roast for dinner,' recalls Thomas Somerville, in his eighteenth-century memoirs.

Geese were *la crème de la crème* for spit-turning, assert Venturus Mandey and J. Moxon in a 1696 book called *Mechanick Powers*. 'If it be need they will continue the labour 12 hours.' After which, presumably, they jumped on the spit and cooked themselves to provide the following night's dinner!

Rather than having a goose loose about the house, clockmakers in Renaissance Italy perfected a more reliable way of driving a spit, and this reached us in the sixteenth century. It was a clockwork jack, driven like a grandfather clock mechanism. A weight was hoisted to

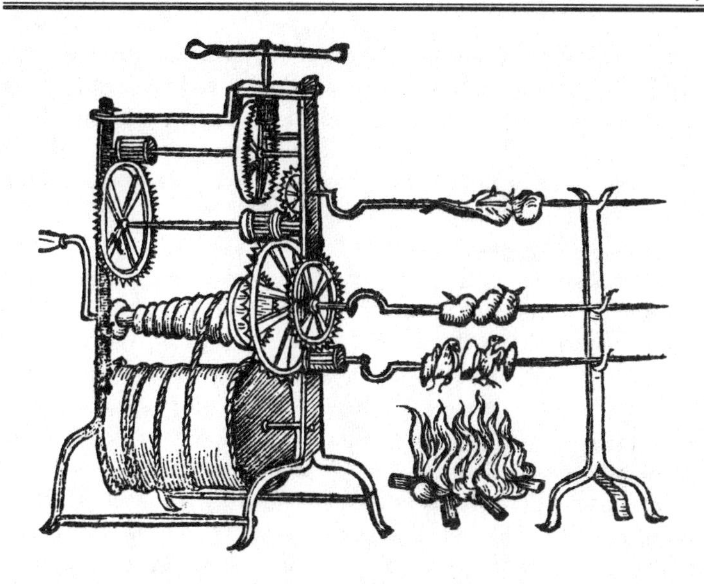

the kitchen ceiling on a pulley and left to fall. Its fall turned a geared wheel connected to a chain which turned the spit. Ivan Day has used one of these. 'I can keep it going for 40 minutes in an 11-foot high kitchen – enough time to roast a chicken,' he says.

Another automatic spit-turner, the Smoke Jack, was a smoke-driven wheel inserted into the chimney and connected to the spit with a contraption of geared wheels. The idea was that the smoke from the fire would make it turn, like a windmill. 'It makes very little Noise, needs no Winding Up, . . . preferable to the more noisy inventions,' enthused John Evelyn in a diary entry in 1675. The downside was that it needed a roaring fire.

Every age has its cooking fads from other countries. The Elizabethans went wild for barbecue grilling – a new and faster way of cooking thinner cuts of meat like chicken wings. Grilling was called carbonado'ing. Like huge collars and silly pointed shoes, it was a fashion that came from our love-hate relationship with the Spanish, who also used to 'carbonado' people as a torture. But the trendy Tudor gentleman would ask his blacksmith to knock up a gridiron, a primitive barbecue which was the epitome of Elizabethan culinary cool. It was an iron frame with close horizontal bars on short legs which also came in handy for standing a boiling pot over the fire.

'The Elizabethans didn't like the charcoal flavour of barbecues, which comes from the fat dripping into the fire and the carbon flying up and searing the meat,' observes Ivan Day. To stop this happening, in 1600, they copied a technique brought back from the Pope's kitchens: covering the meat in heavy paper or putting a 'dripping pan' made of paper beneath it as it cooked. The paper didn't burn because the fire was kept 'quiet' or very low.

By 1720, ordinary fireplaces had a huge array of cooking aids. If you spot these hung up around the inglenooks of old inns, it's a good game to guess what each was used for. Frying pans are easy to recognize. The chimney crane would support a copper kettle with a 'tilter', an excellent safety device which meant that people could tip up pans full of up to 25 pints of boiling water without having to pick them up off the fire.

Spits had acquired a meat-cage in the middle, the metal bars separating and flaring like a balloon egg whisk. This 'cradle' or 'basket' had to be unscrewed to take the meat inside, but once it was there it couldn't slide around and get overdone on one side. It was also considered more hygienic. The meat immediately next to the old, spear kind of spit was not popular in case it was tainted by coming into contact with rust or dirt. Basket-roasting spoiled the look of the meat on the table when the hot bars seared it, so during cooking, it was wrapped in paper or hough pastry, which was taken off during the last stages to brown the outside. Then the meat was 'frothed' with a sprinkling of flour followed by a deluge of fat or batter flavoured with wine, cider, ale, orange or lemon juice. That would bubble into a crust just before serving.

Sometimes, a four-legged dripping pan beneath a roasting joint was filled with batter, so that the juices from the cooking meat would drip into it and make a Yorkshire Pudding at the same time.

If you wanted to cook snacks like herring, sausages or perhaps muffins, you used a toaster. This toasting fork look-alike stood on a metal stand called a trivet, with a dripping pan underneath it. But to toast bread, you slapped the slice between the grids of a rack and used its long handle to hold it against the fire.

For fancy cooking, there were two kinds of wafering iron which cooked a flour, egg and sugar batter sandwiched between their plates heated over the fire. The older, English kind made thin oblong wafers like the ones we eat with ice cream today. The wafer-irons had pretty designs like flowers engraved on them, and the wafers they produced were rolled tightly in a stick shape to eat or made into a cornet shape, tied with ribbons and used as a container for sweets and presents. The second kind of wafering iron had a grid design on it, and cooked Dutch wafers – like thick, American waffles.

To brown the top of cakes and meringues, cooks would use a salamander. This flat circle of iron on a long stick was left in the flames until it became red-hot, then held close to the top of the pie, as modern cooks use a butane jet, to sear it brown.

By the 1800s, joints were hung between the fire and a 'hastener', a metal roasting screen like a fireguard which would reflect heat from the fire back to the joint. If the cook wanted to check the joint's progress, she just opened a door in the screen to look. A special long-handled basting-spoon was made to go through the hole so that she could spoon fat over the joint without moving the whole contraption to get at it.

You would make bread and pastry in a beehive-shaped brick oven set into the sides or back of the fireplaces. Well-off houses had several ovens, and ordinary people could buy earthenware ovens from potters to put in front of the fire. In the 1660s, the upwardly mobile Pepys installed an oven and reported that when his wife tried it for the first time, she burned her pies and tarts.

Poorer people used the village bakehouse. On cookday once a week, there would be a procession of families to the oven. Everyone carried their pies and bread covered with a cloth as in nursery rhyme pictures. Intricate wooden carved stamps would identify each pie's owner. In 'Pat a cake, pat a cake, baker's man,' the baker's man marks the cake with a D 'for baby and me'.

The oven was loaded with brushwood, its door sealed with wet clay to keep the heat in, and the fire lit. Sophisticated ovens had a primitive thermostat called a wise man; a white or black brick which would glow red when the inside was ready. Otherwise, the cook would rely on experience and intuition, double-checking the temperature by throwing a handful of flour in. Once it burned with sparks, that was the signal for the men to rake out the ashes, so the soot wouldn't contaminate the food. This was a dangerous job, but it had to be done meticulously, and finally mopped out with a 'scuffle', a long pole with a sack tied to the end of it. Posher ovens in private houses had a special false floor which could be pulled out to reveal an ash-drawer, where the ash would fall neatly, to be collected and used for scouring and washing.

Quickly, before the heat was gone, the pies and bread were loaded into the oven on 'peels', long-handled wooden spades. One Essex oven still operating in 1890 records cooking times which are the same as today's gas and electric ovens: two hours for a large loaf at the back; two hours for a cake; 25 minutes for buns, put at the front so that they could be taken out ahead of the rest.

In the 1880s, when refrigerated ships brought us cheap Australian mutton and South American beef, people made an effort to afford a Sunday roast dinner, cooked in the bakehouse. It is tempting to look at bakehouses through sepia-coloured glasses, as an ideal of co-operative perfection. As upper-class women complained about bad laundries, lower-class women had bakehouse tales of woe – and there were no consumer laws to protect them.

Bakehouses were only open to suit themselves, and might keep the bread standing around, so that it was spoiled. They could burn or undercook it – no joke when the customer was paying a halfpenny to cook a loaf, at 1849 rates. That doesn't sound much, but the price of bread has always been an emotive subject because it was the staple food of the poor, and because everybody then lived in terror of getting into debt, without state benefits or credit cards. If the bakehouse spoiled the bread, they went hungry.

Cooking at home gave women more control. And the ovens that led to our gas and electric cookers came with the Industrial Revolution.

Cooking with coal

During the 1800s, steam engines, not to mention miners and children working heartbreakingly long hours, hauled coal from the ground so efficiently that our total output rose from ten million tons in 1790 to 240 million tons in 1900.

Coal was king, and it led to those comfortable Victorian kitchens stuffed with cast-iron machines and gadgets. All these kitchen aids could not have been made without coal, because it was the only fuel which burned hot enough to make practical cast iron, rather than the brittle stuff that came out of the charcoal ovens of the past. Things which had been hand-made in wood could now be mass-produced cheaply in cast iron, by machine.

Coal changed the way we cooked, and the look of our home interiors. You needed much less coal than wood to create a roaring fire, so we stopped building wood-burning, huge inglenook fireplaces. Instead, tiny cast-iron fireplaces were installed in the terraced houses built for factory-workers in the 1800s. In older houses, inglenooks were covered up with new cast-iron fireplaces. Not everybody could afford coal to burn in them, though.

In 1900, London coal cost £1 5s a ton, a week's wages for a low-earning man; but near northern mining areas, it was only 10s, with mining families getting 12 tons free a year.

The small fireplaces had no room for a long spit or big cauldron. Joints had to be roasted by hanging them on a hook over the fire, on a clockwork bottle-jack (a roasting gadget shaped like a bottle) and a hastener, the old metal roasting screens. Baking was done in an iron box in front of the fire.

Cast-iron cooking ranges, with several ovens and hobs around a coal fire, came out of inventors' attempts to tidy up the clutter of cooking stands and hooks around the fireplace.

THE PATENT KITCHENER,

A REGISTER COOKING-GRATE, CONSTRUCTED ON NEW AND IMPROVED PRINCIPLES, BY

W. FLAVEL,

IRONMONGER AND COMMISSION AGENT,

BATH-STREET, LEAMINGTON,

AND ADAPTED TO ALL FIRE-PLACES, FROM THREE TO TEN FEET IN LENGTH.

The attention of all housekeepers, and of those who intend to become housekeepers, is earnestly invited to this important article of domestic economy.

It is well adapted for small families, as well as for larger establishments, Inns, and Schools, comprising a Roaster on one side, and an Oven on the other, both of unrivalled excellence; a Hot Plate, Hot Closets, and a Cistern for hot water; a Boiler may also be fixed in the wall behind, or it can be heated at five, ten, or twenty feet from the fire. The Patent Kitchener affords the most ready means of performing in the best manner, either separately or at the same time, all the operations of cookery,—as roasting, baking, boiling, steaming, stewing, &c. with only one fire, and that an open one, which may be of any size, to suit the kitchen of the smallest cottage, or the largest mansion or hotel,—and to prepare a dinner for two or three persons, or for fifty or a hundred.

By no other contrivance can the fire of one grate be made so immediately subservient to the cook's views, and the business of cooking so much facilitated as by this apparatus, which enables the operator to regulate the heat at all times in the nicest manner, without adding to, or diminishing the quantity of fuel in the fire-place.

Its arrangement is so simple, in every department of the culinary process, that servants cannot easily disorder or mismanage it, and the perfect cleanliness attending it cannot fail to be approved by the mistress of an establishment. Its price is moderate, and it is a positive safeguard from the annoyance of smoke.

Two sizes of the Patent Kitchener may be seen as above, in active operation, and it has been adopted in the kitchens of many persons of great knowledge and experience, who have, with much liberality, offered to recommend it to their friends; and, in their respective districts, to permit the proprietor to refer to them for its character and capabilities.

Hot Air Stoves, and Apparatus, for warming and ventilating dwelling houses and other buildings.

Stove Grates, plain and ornamented, constructed on the best principles, for diffusing most heat with smallest consumption of fuel.

Improved Portable Shower Baths, adapted for chambers, &c. &c.

In 1750, the Reverend John Lister, of Shibden Hall in Halifax, installed a very early cast-iron cooker, the Perpetual Oven, for the huge cost of £4 4s. By 1780, the word 'hob' meant a hot area for cooking pans, used in a patent application for a stove by Thomas Robinson of Whitehall. But the range had no one inventor. Ironmongers everywhere were making their own 'open ranges' – an open fire grate surrounded by cast-iron ovens, shelves and burners of all kinds.

Their reasoning was sensible. Everything could be enclosed in a cast-iron 'fire-box' connected to the oven by a flue (large pipe for air and fumes). Rather than having to wait for hot water until the fire was free of cooking clutter, the fire-box would keep everything hot: an oven, kettle and water for washing. It would be easier, cheaper and the food wouldn't get as sooty as it did on an open fire. The hot cast-iron cover would act as a radiator for room heating too. The effect would be like today's Aga and Raeburn stoves.

It was a great idea, but the designs were overcomplicated. The inventors were men, the users mostly women. Perhaps the men didn't talk to the women, or take their needs seriously. Probably, they were so in love with the idea of their new machines that they hoped the cook wouldn't mind putting in the extra muscle-work to fit in with their foibles.

Heaven help the woman who had to cook with crackpot ovens like The Economist, patented in 1770 by a physics professor from Chelsea called Bartholemew Dominiceti. He called it a 'firestove with boilers, pots and other salutory utensils', but it could pass as a rocket ship from Jules Verne's science fiction. There were four ovens and, above these, a hubble-bubble arrangement of six pipes connected by stalks to 18 cooking pots of all sizes, ranged on shelves around the edge of the fire. Although he felt that it 'will be of great utility to His Majesty's subjects in general', it was never heard of again.

An 1813 advertisement from Marriott, a Furnishing Ironmonger of Fleet Street, illustrates a wonderful stove which claims to have self-cleaning saucepans! The writer means that they don't get sooty on the outside – important when they had to be scoured with ashes and sand to clean them. 'Improved Patent Kitchen Range, with Oven, Boiler, Hot Plate, and Hot Closets . . . with a continued supply of 10 gallons of boiling water; the consumption of fuel about half the usual quantity and a certain cure for a Smoky Chimney . . . The vessels are

used without the least soil, and of course, far more durable than those used over common fires.'

Marriott's shop was the Leading Edge of his time, packed with new technology like 'Portable Kitchens of various sizes convenient for Fishing, Sailing and Shooting Parties, which will Bake, Roast, Boil and Steam by one Fire.' Other luxuries include a 'Portable shower bath, enclosed in a wood frame, with curtains and water receiver'. If you were frightened of peeping toms while using it, you could set up Marriott's 'Patent Humane Man Trap' nearby.

By the 1850s, stoves turned into the domestic equivalent of the steam engine with all-conquering names like The Eagle, installed in Sir John Soane's house. They heated water in a samovar-style arrangement with a brass tap at the side. Tea-kettles and saucepans stood in front of the oven doors or at the side, on slot-on iron stands called trivets. Temperature control was basic. To make a small fire to boil a kettle, you pulled in the grate sides (called cheeks). To build up the fire for meat, you folded down the front bars of the grate to enlarge it.

These new ranges were too hot, noisy and sooty to stand in the living room, where the old spit cookery was done, surrounded by the family. So they were installed in another room, where they could smoke without offending anyone: the kitchen. This isolated the cook. The living room changed from a kitchen-diner to a diner-sitting room, and if mother did her own cooking, she was banished to slave over her hot stove alone.

Poorer people had a more sociable time. They still cooked in living rooms, over open fires using hooks and improvised apparatus like the Dutch Oven, a closed metal beehive-shaped oven you stood in front of the fire, which had several shelves and a hook for hanging a roast joint at the top.

A lot of the heat from coal ranges was wasted straight up the chimney. This was observed by an American scientist called Benjamin Thomson, whose good works earned him the German title of Count Rumford. He was obsessive about saving money. In the early 1800s, 'he succeeded in roasting 112 lb of meat in ovens at a cost of fourpence' at London's Foundling Hospital, his proud biographer Frederick Edwards Junior reports with a straight face.

Rumford tried to interest people in energy-saving by insulating their ranges, but it took 40 years for the penny to drop, around 1840. The result was the classic kitchen 'closed range' or close-range seen in period dramas like *Upstairs, Downstairs*. Fires got smaller, and were boxed with a door and top cover, so that the heat had to escape sideways, through the flues, to warm the ovens and water boiler. With their smaller versions known as kitcheners, they offered the first two-speed hobs. Stews could simmer on the hotplate over the fire; but for faster boiling, the top of the hob was taken off, exposing the saucepan to fiercer heat.

Who would think that a cooker could arouse such passion? When closed ranges like the classic Leamington were shown at the Great Exhibition of 1851, people took sides about open or closed ranges as if in a political debate.

For women, cooking with a range was like driving a steam engine, slamming shut a heavy plate or flipping up a series of flues, to get each oven hotter or colder. Closed ranges were fiddly, and each range had individual foibles. Deadly fumes built up if the register, or chimney door, was badly adjusted or made. In 1853, three people died. Knobs and levers were supposed to organize air flows to create steamy ovens for making bread, or dry ovens for pastry.

Instead of one-pot meals, ranges allowed cooks to produce a meal with more and varied dishes: soup, stews, fish, apple pie and custard could be cooked simultaneously, and kept warm easily. But cooks complained that meals tasted of smoke. In 1845, the cookbook writer Eliza Acton noted the strong smell of the ranges, which, 'diffused often entirely through a house, is particularly unpleasant.' Others found the ovens too steamy, because they were so well insulated that air could not escape. Bread 'will be either unevenly baked or altogether burnt,' advised *Lady Bountiful's Legacy* in 1868. Nor were they good for pastry, wrote the chef Jules Goffe in 1867 with Gallic contempt. 'Cast-iron and forged iron ovens may serve well for an army on the move, but I can see no merit in them from the point of view of baking fine quality pastry.'

Soggy pastry! How could British cooking survive that accusation? It didn't. Its reputation rested on meat 'coffined' in crisp pies, and air-roast meat. Meat roasted in an oven is a form of baking, and the taste was different. The best of British cooking was sacrificed to convenience and running hot water, on the iron range, and instead we got overcooked cabbage. The upper classes did not preserve our culinary traditions. Educated by their Grand Tours of Europe, French food was the fashion now, and so much of it that by 1904, a dinner could have 21 courses. We must pay tribute to the cooks who overcame the drawbacks of ranges to cook course after course of consommés, creams, chateaubriands, pommes and tarts.

Iron ranges were handsome beasts, their names proudly picked out in the middle and studded with complex brass knobs, taps and levers. But before they could be lit, they needed someone to clean the flues, sweep out the soot, clear out the ashes (though the lucky ones had a Tidy Betty, a drawer which caught the ashes neatly) and scour inside with soda and hot water.

They could never have survived without large numbers of servants, young girls who got up at dawn to clean and light them, ready to boil water for the mistress's tea in bed and the master's bath before serving a hot breakfast at 8.30 a.m. In 1851, 13 per cent of our workforce were in service in England and Wales. After the early-morning routine came the dreaded daily polishing with black lead, to stop the range rusting in the steamy kitchen atmosphere. If there was no maid, this ate into the cook's time so much that the cooking suffered. No wonder that the first convenience foods appeared, like custard powder, self-raising flour and sauces like ketchup.

Black-leading the stove was a skill. The lead came wrapped in a sausage-shaped paper. The brands were called Zebo (with a zebra picture on the cover), Nixey, Lion and The Rising Sun. The maid

had to break off a nugget and mix it with water using a little round brush. It was like making cake-icing with sugar and water. Too much water and it dripped down over the floor; too little and it clogged the brush.

She applied it, polished, then shined the handles with emery paper. The tap on the water container was brass polished, and the hearth was whitened with Hearth's Heart Stone, rubbed on with a wet cloth. When that was finished, that left only the fire tongs, poker, rake and shovel to rub and shine with emery paper.

As for the middle-class Victorians, who could afford several servants but helped out occasionally themselves, the stove was a mixed blessing, as the cooking arrangements of the writer Thomas Carlyle show. In 1834, Carlyle and his wife Jane rented their house in Chelsea at £35 a year. One room had a large hearth equipped with cooking equipment: 'Swing trivets, fall-down bar, sliding hobs, winder racks and underslide' in the landlord's proud description. The Carlyles ignored this and used an open kitchen range in the front kitchen which integrated the old and the new, and suited their porridge and mutton chops. There was a built-in oven, and a chimney crane, sliding hook for a stewpot over the fire, and meat-roasting jack.

For Carlyle, who was notoriously stingy, the lure of the new closed ranges must have been huge. By 1852, he parted with £7 3s on a new range from Edinburgh which heated a constant flow of 2 gallons of hot water on tap, piped from a small cistern in a cupboard nearby. It probably consumed 10 tons of coal a year and was none too clean. Soot-soiled pots and pans were kept in a cupboard with the shelves painted black to disguise the dirt which built up – partly because Jane Carlyle would only allow one candle in the gloomy kitchen. The work it created contributed to the departure of 22 cooks and housemaids from that year until the amiable Jane's death in 1866.

Smoke from the ranges affected the environment. Every town had chest-tightening smog, caused not so much by tall factory chimneys as continual smoke from lower house chimneys. Disaster was averted by the coming of smokeless fuel. As coal-mining technology progressed, the deeper seams of coal produced a hard, slow-burning coal called anthracite which produced very little smoke, could burn all night and so did not need so much ash-raking or flue-cleaning. In 1882, the earliest anthracite-burning stove, the Treasure, was displayed at the Exhibition of the Smoke Abatement Society. The Marquis of Lorne, opening the show, said: 'Were the public but to avail themselves of such appliances, we might one day see roses blooming in Kensington Gardens.' In 1907, among advertisements in Mrs Beeton, The Wilson Patent Portable Cooking Range claimed to 'consume smoke'. Or you could use something like the Imp Soot Destroyer – a mysterious box which claimed 'carries away the soot for 4d' from Gourmet and Co Home Necessities.

Cast-iron ranges are seen now as a symbol of a happy Victorian family home with warmth and puddings aplenty. They were convenient, with their hot water heaters, and if they meant more work, most women who could afford them had servants to do it.

They were also the most disastrous kitchen machines invented. They burdened servants, made our cooking worse, isolated women at home, where they 'slaved all day over a hot stove,' a phrase they added to the language. Their smoke and fumes affected our health, made buildings filthy and blighted our greenery. We still feel their effect in our climate, as the sulphur dioxide they puffed into the sky helped to erode the ozone layer.

But now we don't have to use them, we can appreciate the ingenuity of the Victorians, and their fun side. Portable closed ranges were an American idea, based on a room-heater invented by Benjamin Franklin in the 1780s and used in the Civil War. They were not portable as we understand it. Big insulated iron boxes, you needed a horse and wagon to haul them around. In 1841, a Scotsman called James Smith brought the idea back from America, set up a factory with a childhood friend, Stephen Wellstood, and by 1912, their stoves were used all over the British Empire.

There were 200 Smith & Wellstood designs, reflecting changing tastes of the century from the heavy-hinged gothic 'Mistress', to the

curly art nouveau 'Sultana'. Every cooking need was catered for by stoves designed to go everywhere from a luxury yacht to a desert train, and for value, they were the Littlewoods of their day. In 1885, a long, low oblong stove called The Enchantress came with two iron pots, two frying pans, eight baking pans, a large ham boiler, a tea kettle, a potato steamer and a gridiron, all for £3 3s; water boiler extra.

Coal ranges were the norm until 1914. People went on buying them until the 1940s, hoping to retain a home-sweet-home aura in a drastically changing world. Having a coal range was a sign of conservative values, and was also an upper class habit which came from practical need in their country homes, with no gas or electricity for miles. The Carron range, advertised in the 1920s in *The Lady* magazine, had a modern glass oven door and was 'by appointment' to the King.

When gas and electric cookers came in, coal came out with identical cookers which burned coal, like the Briffo, extolled by its makers Crittall Cookers in *Country Life* in 1935. In this extraordinary gas cooker clone, the coal was contained in a 'Magic Bowl' inside the oven door. 'This bowl is so small that it only consumes 15 lb of coal a day and makes economy compulsory,' reads the advert, which claims that you can 'cook for 2d to 3d a day.' The ashes dropped automatically into a special tray inside (really collects all the ash and prevents any dust or dirt in the kitchen).

Other 1930s new coal ranges fitted into a fireplace, but look hopelessly clumsy, with the modern wipe-clean enamel finishes of gas and electric ovens. 'The Thompsons decided on a Triplex,' proclaimed an advertisement in *Good Housekeeping* in 1936, adding that 200,000 Triplex ranges had been sold. 'They are careful, critical people are the Thompsons. Want to know every why and wherefore before they buy. But in TRIPLEX they found all the answers to happy living.'

Their new purchase has a tiny fire with a shelf for two saucepans in front of it, two ovens, a water boiler and a backaching, finger-frying floor-level grill. Mrs Thompson probably kept an electric kettle and hotplate in the cupboard without telling her husband.

The cooker which kept alive the coal-burning oven in our kitchens is the Aga. Invented in 1922 by a Swedish Nobel-prize winning physicist, Dr Gustaf Dalen after he had been blinded by a laboratory explosion, it reached Britain in 1929. A huge fire-box which burns day and night at a controlled 900 degrees centigrade, its 6 inches of heavy insulation was

Mr. BRIFFO says

Change to a *really clean* COOKER

and cook for **2d.** *to* **3½d.** *a day*

From the day you install a Briffo you start to save. But that's not all. Your meals are better cooked—for everybody's agreed that there's nothing to beat the even healthy heat of coal for cooking. Your kitchen becomes a pleasanter place—the Briffo concentrates the heat where it is wanted—in the hotplate and the oven. It is simple to light—simple to clean. No fumes—no dirt—and the ashes drop into a special ash-tray *inside* the cooker. Read the 8 advantages—and remember this modern economical cooker can be installed for **25/- PER MONTH**

so effective that it used a fraction of the coal burned by the old ranges. In 1938, it guaranteed not to cost more than £10 a year in coal, while the Aga 'for the smaller house' promised to reduce the fuel bill to £1 per quarter.

The Aga's hallmarks are its lidded hobs, one for boiling, one for simmering, which take three pans each. There are also two ovens, one kept constantly hot, one cooler, and a warming closet which farmers' wives could use to dry out shivering orphan lambs, whilst roasting a nice leg of lamb for lunch above them.

Although expensive and costly to install, Agas were sold to last a lifetime and save such amounts of fuel that it 'bought itself'. Embraced by the land-owning classes, now feeling the pinch after the introduction of income tax, for their country houses not connected to gas or

electricity, Agas became a silent but telling indicator of social class. 1930s advertisements show its owners in ballgowns and fox-hunting outfits rather than aprons, and suggest that Agas will help you keep the servants happy. *Country Life*, in 1938, carries a recommendation from the fierce-looking Compton Mackenzie, writer of *Whisky Galore*. 'The Aga which was installed in my house on the island of Barra two years ago has burned steadily night and day ever since . . . My Siamese cats consider the top, covered with a blanket, provides them with the finest lodging outside Siam.'

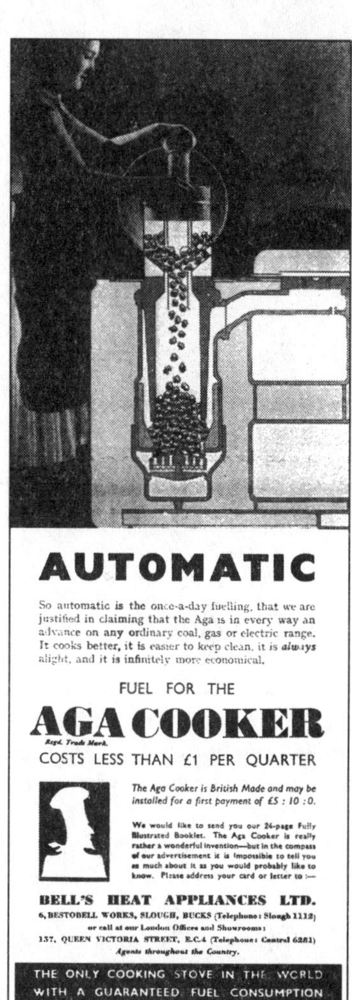

In the last 28 years, Aga has rocketed to the status of a design and class icon, synonymous with the luxury country kitchen epitomized by Smallbone's craftsman-made fitted wooden fitted kitchens. Aga found new buyers in townies who wanted its 'country' appeal in their kitchens. These fashion-conscious middle class people didn't need it to run the house heating too, because they already had electric central heating. So to appeal to them, in 1980 Aga revamped itself, introducing colours like electric blue, and gas or electric options.

The progress of Aga has been observed by Ian Simpson, a property developer who for 20 years has renovated Cotswold farmhouses with the most luxurious kitchens. A £750,000 house would sell because it had an Aga. 'There are various names an

estate agent will think worth mentioning on the sale particulars – Aga, Miele dishwashers and En Tout Cas tennis courts,' he says.

It wasn't that people demanded a lot of their cooker. Many of the houses were used as weekend homes. But in the wealthy 1980s, people bought things not to fulfil a need, but by designer labels. Aga was the 'right' name in the kitchen just as Armani was the 'right' name in clothes. Even when the recession hit, appearances had to inspire confidence. 'Agas appealed to my customers and still do,' assesses Ian. 'But they made kitchens too hot in summer, and we had to provide other means for people to cook, so we added built-in ovens and ceramic hobs. The problem is, the whole kitchen is taken up with cooking surfaces.'

As the 1990s emphasized 'caring', the Aga proved popular as the embodiment of a warm, loving home. With less money around, it had to earn its keep by becoming more practical for everyday cooking. 'Now Aga has moved to the electric oven and the ceramic top attached, and we put those in,' says Ian. 'These new ones look old-fashioned; in fact half is Aga, half electric cooker and halogen hobs. Expensive, though. Not much change from £6,500.'

The latest Aga can be gold-plated, for an extra £750. It is perhaps the ultimate irony that the last cooker in a line of those invented to save pennies on fuel, has become such a costly status symbol.

Cooking with gas

The first recorded gas cooker was a natural gas spring near Wigan, Lancashire. People boiled eggs over it in 1687. But nobody considered seriously cooking with gas until 1824, 17 years after street lighting was first installed in Brighton and Holborn. Those early gas flames were adjusted to burn cool, to make them safe inside glass shades, and gas had been thought not hot enough to cook with.

It was a good fry-up that changed history. Workers at the Aetna Iron Works near Liverpool took a shotgun barrel, piped gas through it and punched holes along it to let the flames burn through. Then they fried a meal over it. This gun-barrel, twisted into a circle, formed the basis of the gas ring we use today. It was quickly taken up by restaurants as a quick way of cooking chops and steaks. Gas flames were easily turned on and off, and were hotter and faster than the radiant heat from the hobs of a coal range.

There was only one problem: gas stank. Early gas, made by burning coal, was different from our cleaner, all but odourless and safer natural gas from under the sea. A cartoon by Isaac Cruikshank headed 'The Good Effects of Carbonic Gas!!!' shows a woman shouting from her window above a gas light: 'What the Devil are you Funking us all with your stinky smoake!' A visit to the Gas Gallery at Manchester's Museum of Science and Industry, where gas lights burn, will convince anyone of the alarming smell.

But the success of any new breakthrough depends on obsessive visionaries. James Sharp, who worked at Northampton Gas Works, put those gas burners into the bottom of ovens and by 1830, he was making and selling the first gas cookers. They were small cast-iron boxes with no shelves, just a hook like a roasting-jack to hang roasting meat at the top of the oven. The on-switch was at the side and you lit the oven with one of the newly invented matches. Oddly, he didn't put more gas burners on top to make a complete cooker, so users could only bake and roast. When a middle-class income started on £300 a year and gas was 15s a cubic foot, that made them a luxury.

Every new cooker-maker seeks a top chef to recommend it. Gas scored a major publicity coup when Alexis Soyer installed gas cookers and burners in the new kitchen of London's Reform Club in 1840. Soyer was a superchef who escaped to London from the 1830 French revolution, when he dodged a mob by jumping on his kitchen table and singing *La Marseillaise*. His brother, chef to the Duke of Cambridge, introduced him to top tables, and Alexis took advantage of the exclusive gas pipes in Pall Mall. Gas kept his kitchen 'as white as a young bride,' as one journalist remarked.

But his oven would never have caught on. It looked like a giant tiered cake-table. The gas made a halo-shaped fire inside the base. You put the food on to each shelf and covered the whole thing with a steel cylinder. There was no way of controlling the heat or checking the food without unsheathing the whole oven. But to prove that it worked, in 1846 Soyer cooked a banquet culminating in a pyramid of meringue 1½ feet high, decorated with a portrait of the guest of honour's father, a 'subtlety' that any Tudor cook would have appreciated.

Despite his efforts, gas cookers didn't set the world on fire. The organizers of the 1851 Great Exhibition made sure of that, by banning them from its line-up of all that was supposed to be newest and best. This ban was put down to prejudice, but the show's organizer Prince Albert was no fuddy-duddy. They probably feared an explosion ripping through the glass exhibition centre, with its thousands of visitors in Hyde Park, not far from Buckingham Palace. Not to mention dozens of fragile ladies fainting from the smell. Their scepticism is understandable in the face of whacky inventions like the Wooden Gas Stove of 1850. This metal-lined box had its burners tucked away on the inside of the oven door for more oven space – absolutely lethal for cooks in long skirts!

The Gasfitters Mutual Association reacted to the ban by holding their own show that year. It starred James Sharp's biggest cooker, which

was more like a fairground attraction than anything an ordinary person might want at home. It was a cylinder, 1½ metres wide, with the gas burning in a ring on the oven floor. Joints hung from a hook at the top, and above the meat was a clever little second oven for pastry. Above that a huge water-heater, six big pots and seven smaller saucepans were stacked precariously on them. Some 800 people watched Sharp demonstrate his oven in a lecture called Gas-tronomy. Then he cooked supper for 120 on the lecturing table: 34 lb of roast beef, 24 lb of boiled mutton, with cod, eight plum puddings and trimmings, 'the dripping collected being valued at two shillings.' How like those thrifty early oven makers to squeeze a profit from a demonstration!

Over the next 50 years, while coal ranges became more elaborate, gas ovens quietly assumed the form we know today. Glass oven doors appeared in 1855; oven shelves in 1860; and, at last, gas burners on top in 1866. In 1893, John Wright & Co produced a two-speed burner, with a separate inner and an outer burner. For simmering, you turned one on; for boiling, you used both.

The Great Exhibition relented and showed a gas oven in 1861, mounted on a stone slab as a fire precaution. Spectators judged it noisy and dirty. The smell would get into the food, making it taste strange, and poison them. Even after the smell had lessened, when boffins in the 1870s mixed more air with the gas, the myth of gas-flavoured food remained. One gourmet announced that 'the flavour of meat roasted by plain gas was decidedly better than that of the meat roasted by atmospheric (air-mixed) gas.'

An engraved advertisement for Metropolitan Gas Stoves was probably one of the first tries at selling kitchen machines using an attractive girl. It seemed to try to appeal to the servant, who might ask her employers to buy her the cooker. Or maybe the master would have been interested. It showed a young cook in pleated cap, her apron tied under her bustle and seven rows of frills beneath, in the fashion of 1870. The message was that she had time to frou-frou herself up because her new gas oven needed so little attention compared with coal. She was stirring a bubbling pot, paying no attention to a full bucket of hot water gushing out from the gas oven's boiler. The oven door was open to cool it down now that cooking was nearly finished, since there were no thermostats to control the cooking temperature. The cat was about to investigate a mouthwatering meal of a pie and soufflé on the top shelf, a joint hanging from a hook and two chickens roasting, the grease dripping down to a slide-out tray at the oven bottom. Plates were warming next to a grill tray.

Those in no position to complain were experimented on. Despite fears of poisoned food, gas was first used for the masses in hospital cooking from about 1870. The Smoke Abatement Society backed gas in its 1882 exhibition, showing the lavish and imaginative ovens of William Sugg. These are visions of heaven. His Cordon Bleu of 1884 had three ovens with glass doors, including one copper-lined for bread and pastry; two water-powered turning spits inside his 'Parisienne Roaster' and six hobs supporting 12 saucepans. Affordable by people like the Duke of Westminster, an early convert to gas whose iron-lined brick pastry oven was so good, it was a national affront to the French, according to a top chef called Alfred Suzanne. 'It is surprising that France, the culinary nation *par excellence*, has allowed herself to be outdistanced by England in the construction of gas cooking apparatus,' he wrote after seeing it.

As coal begrimed our cities, people realized the virtues of gas. There was no heavy coal to carry in, no smoke or soot to be cleaned by sad little boys sent (and sometimes fatally stuck) up a chimney, and no ashes to be raked out each day. Servants didn't have to rise at dawn to light the range. Unlike a coal range, gas didn't need checking and feeding to stop it going out, and it didn't make the kitchen a sweatshop on hot days. In 1890, enough people had bought gas stoves to justify the oven-maker Sugg's daughter Marie Jenny writing the first gas cookery book, *The Art of Cooking by Gas*.

Some carped that gas shrank the food. Mrs Beeton put paid to the idea. Her 1907 *Household Management* said: 'It has been shown that

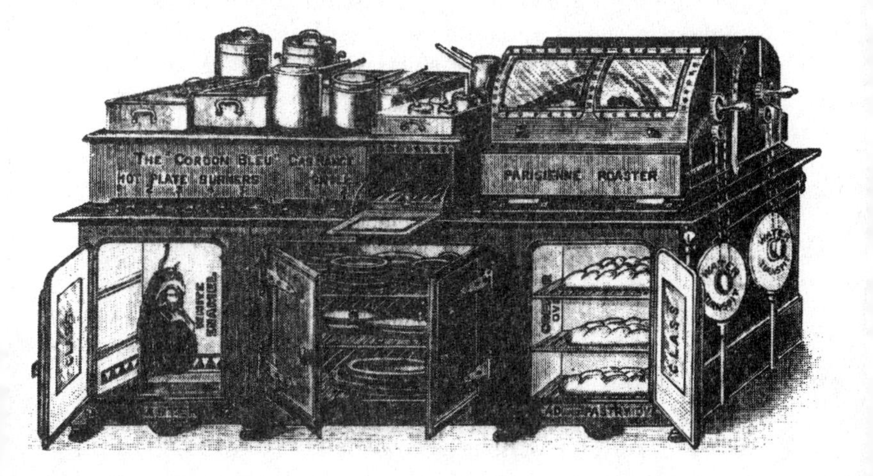

meat cooked in a coal-heated oven loses about 35 per cent of its weight; in a gas oven only 25 per cent,' though she advised stacking some bricks in the oven bottom to make it more airtight for pastry. If you still weren't sure, an advertisement in the same edition announced the Trident, a 'combined gas and coal oven, to be used with gas or fire at option. Always ready for either.'

The small size of gas ovens suited the working classes. They fitted perfectly into their sculleries – long thin back rooms intended for washing – introduced around 1870. The gas pipe which powered the oven could be unpopped to power a boiler for hot water too.

But few could afford gas until 1890, when Parkinson & W.B. Cowan invented the first pre-payment slot meter to go inside people's homes, and offered cookers for hire. Few inventions made such a dramatic difference. Now, nobody needed to worry about running into debt. They could put a penny in the slot and pay as they cooked. By 1900, two million homes cooked with gas. The health of the working classes improved because, for the first time, children could have regular hot meals cooked easily and cheaply.

By the 1900s, gas cookers were no longer clones of coal ranges. They were smaller and lighter, and they seemed to be made for a different race from the generously proportioned Edwardians. In 1907, the latest coal-burning Russell's Patent Lifting Fire Herald Range offered two ovens, four hobs, a huge plate rack and four hot shelves – plenty of space to cook an eight-course Edwardian dinner including turtle soup, stuffed cock's combs, breast of pigeon, and plovers' eggs. You couldn't manage such magnificence on the Planet, produced the same year, with two burners, a small grill and one oven with three shelves. Those gas cookers, with their flimsy ovens lined with enamel or tiles, signalled the end of Edwardian grand cooking. By 1924, their roast pheasant had turned into the 'typical dinner' cooked by *Good Housekeeping* as a test: roast beef, Yorkshire pudding, roast potatoes, cauliflower in white sauce, gravy, fruit pie and custard.

It was becoming clear that electric street-lighting had taken over from gas. Gas companies suddenly woke up to their future, as a cooking and heating fuel. To survive, they had to produce more advanced gas cookers. Cooks had to throw flour inside an oven to check its heat. If the flour went dark brown, the oven was the right temperature for pastry; if it went light brown, it was fine for scones. In 1923,

Radiation Ltd invented the thermostat that controls oven heat, the Regulo which we still use to set the oven temperature. They went overboard, with 15 different heat settings.

'Servants are as scarce as blackberries in May,' wrote Beryl F. Dupigny in *Good Housekeeping* after the 1914–18 war. From two and a half million before the war, there were under a million servants in 1919. Good cooks were particularly scarce, and suddenly-servantless ladies were not prepared to use the ranges they had inflicted on their staff. They had never been taught to cook, and there were no ready-prepared meals from Marks & Spencer.

As their husbands took refuge in boarding-school stodge at their clubs, ladies searched for a fail-safe cooker. New World Radiation cookers advertised this as if it were a robot cook. 'Mrs Bonny' advises a young wife whose husband has stormed off: 'My dear, I'm quite sure he's feeling very sorry for what he said. You'll make it up all right. Look after his meals. It makes such a difference to a man. You just choose from the Radiation Cookery Book the dinner you think you would like. Then you give it to the cooker to cook . . . You come back at the right time and you find every single thing just done to a nicety . . . Richard will be saying your cooking reminds him of his mother's.'

Cleaning the oven was another chore. Black-leading was out of the question. Wipe-down glass enamelling was perfected around 1915, but at first it cost so much that it was only used inside ovens. All-enamelled cookers were introduced by R & A Main in 1927. The eggshell-effect speckles of green, blue and grey made black cast iron look dirty by comparison. 1928 'gas ranges' reflected a craze for all things Chinese, with 'gay new shades' like Mandarin Red and Jade Green.

Those early cookers, with names like the Improved Mentor, the Puritan and the Bachelor Griller, were helpfully designed, with plate-racks, splashbacks and slide-out oven shelves. Cooker tops generally had three burners, not four. The grill was cunningly designed to double as a big middle burner.

Peta Flint still cooks with a 1930s New World Radiation stove, found on a dump in pristine condition. 'It has three little hobs and a grill underneath, but the heat from the grill comes up through the middle of the hobs and I can use it as an extra burner at the same time,' she explains. 'It's blue-grey enamel with brass switches. The regulos aren't very good. You have to put them higher to get the right heat. When I found it, it was so heavy that the roof of my car caved in when I put it on the roof-rack.'

Economy was important. *The Daily Mail Cookery Book* of 1927 suggests batch cooking: having only one or two 'cooking mornings' each week and re-heating cooked food on other days. *The Housewife's ABC* of 1921 recommends finishing off partly-cooked food like porridge by leaving it all night in a box packed with hay as a natural slow cooker. Other cooking aids grew up around gas, like

Cooking won't keep me out of the garden

I'm a regular 'REGULO' fan!

I'm proud of my garden and it takes up a lot of my time—too much time if it wasn't for my 'Regulo' controlled cooker! I just set the 'Regulo' control, pop the meal into the oven—and then I'm off into the garden for a good bout of tidying up. The meal cooks itself . . . perfectly! . . . and I don't have to keep dashing indoors for fear something has gone wrong. I know I can trust the 'Regulo' to look after the cooking.

Goodness! I'd no more go back to the old way than I'd abandon my lawn mower for a scythe.

REGULO

This Radiation "Regulo" Cooking Timer enables you to time exactly any cooking operation Bell rings at end of cooking time. Simple to use. Obtainable at Gas Showrooms.

The 'Regulo' Cooking Numbers appear in the triangular opening as the knob is turned. The three sides of the triangle are a reminder of the features that have made the New World the most perfect cooking oven obtainable, i.e., single oven burner, direct-bottom-flue-outlet, and the 'Regulo' automatic heat control. These three together ensure perfect cooking, and are only obtainable in the New World Gas Cooker.

NEW WORLD

REGULO-CONTROLLED PORCELAIN ENAMELLED

GAS COOKERS

SEE THEM AT YOUR GAS SHOWROOMS

Post under ½d. stamp

To Radiation Ltd., (Dept. 828/7)
164, Queen Victoria Street, London, E.C.4
Please send me your free Booklet, "Better Breakfasts."

NAME ....

ADDRESS ....

COUPON

MADE BY Radiation

"REGULO" IS THE REGISTERED TRADE MARK OF RADIATION LTD.

the Nobby Frying Pan, an extraordinary thing covered in lumps which claimed to halve your gas bill and was 'guaranteed not to burn' according to the advert.

By the mid-1930s, electric cookers challenged gas. They were much more expensive, but they had pre-set timers which could turn the oven on while you were out – and some could even turn each hob on and off too. It sounds fine in principle, but in practice, one can imagine coming home to chaos, since electricity still had no reliable thermostat and real cooks know that cooking is never an exact science.

Gas couldn't self-light because pilot-lights had yet to be invented. But it fought back by emphasizing its regulo thermostat system. Walt Disney films were the cinema hits of the time, and gas advertising went through a vogue for cartoon characters like Mrs Adjusto or Mr Therm, a red man with a head made of flame, who offered to take care of your cooking. 'Going Walks? I'll come – wait till I set the oven on control,' says the woman to her husband in a 1936 ad, at the height of the fashion for fresh air.

Consumer power was rising, and makers tried to appear sympathetic to women. The Vulcan offered a 'housewife-planned hotplate' – the Parkinson Flag, a lid that doubled as a worksurface. In 1936, gas cookers moved their controls to the front from the sides. 'If women had earlier been allowed a voice in design, this improvement would

have come years ago,' wrote Helen Venner in the staunchly pro-electric *Good Housekeeping*.

Then the first modern-looking white steel cooker appeared in 1937. Parkinson's Renown was based on a special model 'chosen for the kitchen of the KING'S HOUSE' as the advertisement in 1935's *Illustrated London News* trumpeted. (This was a complete house given to George V for his Silver Jubilee by all the Royal Warrant-holders.) It was such a crowd-puller at the Ideal Home Exhibition that it was put on the market as 'the cooker of one's dreams', a clever buzzphrase at a time when Freud's dream analysis was all the rage. Who knows what strange sexual undercurrents Freud would find in a woman who dreamed of a cooker?

People wanted light, cleanliness and ease after the dark days of the war and the financial depression. Small kitchen conveniences appeared. Kleenoff paint-on oven-cleaner arrived (10d a tin, no scrubbing). Phoenix Improved Oven Glass Dishes, designed by a woman, Elizabeth Craig, matched your shiny white cooker, with 'no crevices to hold grease or dirt' and 'rims constructed to hold pastry firmly'.

By 1939, three-quarters of all British families had a gas cooker and, unlike oil and coal, gas was not rationed during the war, which left those unconnected to gas, in areas like Norfolk, out in the cold. Few immediately replaced their old cookers with white ones. This wasn't an age that replaced machines on a whim. They waited until they broke down beyond repair.

In the 1940s, an aerial view of British kitchens would reveal a fair number of old cast-iron ovens, and lots of coloured enamel. Poorer people, who hired rather than bought cookers, could update faster, perhaps to the latest New World self-lighting cookers, which lit the burners from a pilot light in the centre. Each burner was connected to the light with a tiny pipe, and when it was switched on, the gas from the burner reached the pilot to ignite it. The pilot light meant that gas cookers could have auto-timers too. In 1949, the American Stove Company was advertising Magic Chef. 'Girls, it's simply a matter of timing,' smiles the cutie who has been shopping for a new hat but has still managed to produce dinner for her husband on time, using the automatic on/off switches on the hobs and ovens.

'You always knew when someone used gas because you could smell it as you knocked on the front door,' reflects vintage gas cooker expert James Bunce. The Dutch discovered natural gas under the North Sea in the 1940s and in 1967, gas engineers began visiting each home to convert cookers to this less smelly and less dangerous gas. Natural gas was not lethal, and newspapers no longer carried tales of depressed housewives who had killed themselves with their heads in the oven. In 1969, electric Piezo spark ignition, with safe audible clicking to show that it was working, replaced the pilot light.

The best-selling cooker of all was Parkinson's Prince. Introduced in 1958, it had a new 'eye level grill', as well as burners with different heats. It reigned during the dowdiest period of all, when cooking was unpopular among swinging chicks of the sixties and liberated ladies of the seventies. Then came built-in kitchens. Gas ovens were slow to produce desirable cookers. In its first assessment of built-in cookers in March 1978, the Consumers' Association magazine *Which?* pointed out that many built-in gas ovens had no grill.

Built-in kitchens allowed gas and electric ovens to charge top-whack prices for cookers that had less 'features' than ever, not even legs and frames. But people exchanged shelves, warming ovens and other conveniences for good looks.

Built-in kitchens blurred the old rivalry between gas and electricity. No longer did you buy either all-gas or all-electric at the Gas or Electricity Showroom. She who chose a Neff electric oven could also have a Creda gas hob.

But a different kind of built-in gas cooker emerged as kitchen designer Johnny Grey, working for Smallbone fitted kitchens, promoted the idea of the Unfitted Kitchen from the mid-1980s. This idealized old-fashioned kitchens, tapping a backlash of feeling against built-in which had its roots in a revulsion in the British

character against the over-perfect.

Gas cooker sales soared during the 1980s after a surge of interest in cooking which made chefs TV stars. Natural gas was seen as ecologically superior to electricity after nuclear power stations that produced electricity were suspected of causing leukaemia and other illnesses.

First came industrial gas cookers. Restaurant kitchens had never lost their preference for gas cooking. Their heavy, stainless steel cookers were favoured by male graphic designers moving into converted warehouses in London's Docklands. They were a reaction against streamlined, built-in cookers, they looked good in large, open spaces, and they gave the impression that the owner had a 'serious' approach to food and knew something about cooking that the rest of us didn't. These cookers were hard to use and showed every fingerprint, but that didn't matter to the owner, who usually had no children and ate mostly in exclusive restaurants.

Ironically, industrial chic as a style originated among the poor in the early 1980s, when social changes created a drifting underclass. Hotel kitchens provided casual work, and some furnished their squats with the throw-outs they found there. The idea of 'found' machinery fitted with the middle class's growing concern with recycling, and from there it found its way to Docklands.

The polar opposite of the industrial gas cooker was the nostalgic, vaguely Victorian-looking double oven gas range, which appeared in the late 1980s. Sculleries were knocked into sitting rooms to make big kitchen/diners. Double ovens were desirable, since sit-down family meals were increasingly replaced by ad hoc snacking, and people on diets from F-plan to high-protein demanded totally different meals. Families in period houses liked the nostalgic feel of Aga cookers but they were expensive and they felt they wanted a traditional controllable cooker, rather than the Aga's constantly-on, pre-set ovens and hobs.

'We launched Rangemaster in 1995,' says Jill Walton, Marketing Manager for Flavel Leisure, whose founders, the Flavel family, originally dealt in gunpowder and then invented the Kitchener coal range. 'The single cooker size version is the country's top-selling cooker; the double range is the third best-selling. What we have now is the traditional look with shiny rich colours with griddles and features, and now we're bringing out a black one but without the black leading.' The Rangemaster is typical of the new gas cooker because it mixes gas and electricity: next to a cast-iron gas griddle is an electric plate-warmer. Cookers are no longer all-gas or all-electric but, like built-in ovens and hobs, they can be bought with hobs and ovens using any combination of gas or electricity.

Foodies, with families or friends to impress during the new informal kitchen-centred dinner parties, settled in the

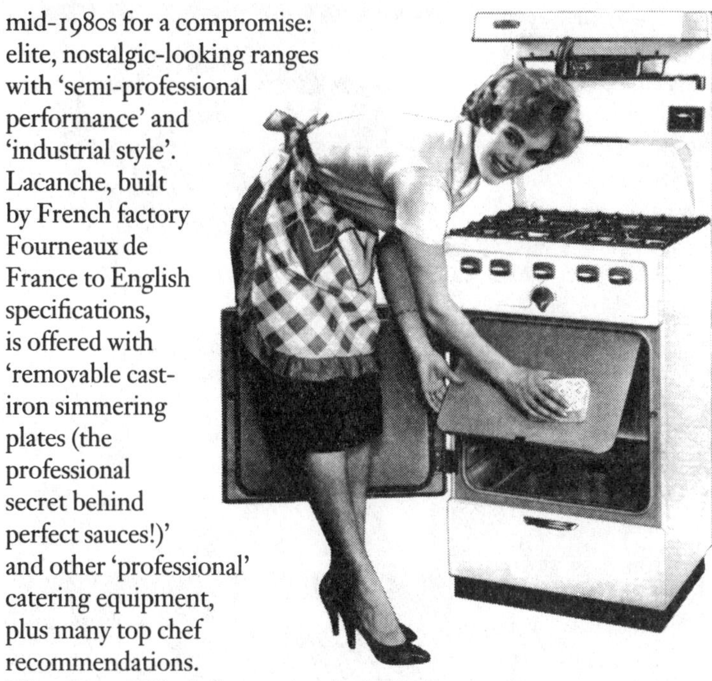

mid-1980s for a compromise: elite, nostalgic-looking ranges with 'semi-professional performance' and 'industrial style'. Lacanche, built by French factory Fourneaux de France to English specifications, is offered with 'removable cast-iron simmering plates (the professional secret behind perfect sauces!)' and other 'professional' catering equipment, plus many top chef recommendations. The ghost of Alexis Soyer, the chef who first used gas 150 years ago, still walks the restaurant kitchens of London.

Cooking with electricity

In 1882, when electric lights first appeared in ordinary homes, the huge connection fee made it affordable only for the rich. Hostesses engraved 'electricity' on their invitations to entice their friends to goggle at the new invisible force.

At a gathering of electrical engineers in 1885, someone suggested cooking with electricity and was squashed. How could you cook on something that had no flame? The brighter sparks among them fiddled around, trying to cook chickens over electric bulbs and running wires between double-skinned metal boxes, until H.F. Dowsing demonstrated a prototype electric cooker at Crystal Palace's exhibition hall in 1891. Two years later, his cooker was put on the market by Crompton & Company, owned by his electric-mad friend Colonel Crompton.

These early ovens look like cast-iron safes: huge boxes with the knobs at the side and no hobs. They were small, because unlike gas and coal, they didn't need large amounts of combustible air inside. But they followed the design of coal and gas ranges 'as', said one maker, Carron, 'an unfamiliar appearance might alarm servants.'

More worrying were the sparks and hums. Early ovens like the 1912 Carron had their controls mounted on the wall behind them, so the cook had to reach dangerously over the hot pots to get to them. One owner warned the servants not to dowse the controls with water, 'no matter the provocation'. Worse were electric shocks. Today's plugs are three-pin because they contain a connection to earth, which guards against electric shock. Until the 1930s, plugs were two-pin because the Institute of Electrical Engineers advised against the safety device of connecting to an earth terminal. They felt this guarded against the risk of damaging the machine with an electric fault, never mind whether the user was killed.

Something about electricity inspired electricians to convert the world to it, with a semi-religious zeal. Anything gas could do, electricity set out to do better. Hotels used gas jets to grill and fry. So electric cooker companies copied the idea, with hotplates, frying pans and all sorts of mini-cookers, heated 'invisibly' by an element (a heat-making coil of wires) in the base. Without thermostats to keep the temperature down, the elements overheated, especially if a saucepan overboiled on them. Because they were embedded in a solid base, they couldn't be fixed.

The electric cooker companies were undeterred by a little thing like machines that didn't work very well. No other utility has understood the value of publicity so well, or thought so big. Where the gas people cautiously issued a cookbook when they had sold enough cookers to justify it, the electricity people opened a cookery school in 1895, two years after the first cooker had been sold.

Whether or not people went for serious lessons at The School of Electric Cookery, the demure proprietress, Margaret Fairclough, gained huge attention. The *Black and White* magazine dubbed it 'the school with trained lightning' in a gushy description. While Margaret rolled pastry at an ordinary table, six appliances cooked things 'without any fire, or apparent signs of heat'. A kettle boiled; a 'fluted griller' was 'cooking gaily away with an independent air'. 'On the hot plate, scones were toasting; in a frying pan, potatoes were frying; while the little pots were occupied with stewing birds and simmering jam.'

The chef Alexis Soyer had praised gas. So The City of London Electric Lighting Company got a cook called Mathieu Williams to endorse electricity. People were urged to see the new machines demonstrated daily in the showrooms. In 1894, the Company held an 'All-Electric Banquet', at which 120 guests consumed turtle soup, three kinds of fish, veal, chops, roast duckling, asparagus and Charlotte Russe cooked with patchy success in six ovens. And like gas cookers, electric cookers were offered for hire, at 7s a quarter.

Queen Victoria was impressed. An all-electric kitchen was fitted into her royal yacht, with ovens, soup and coffee boilers, hotplates and grills run from its own generator. Others followed her lead: the Bank of England, Harvey Nichols and the Duke of Westminster in Grosvenor House. Torquay opened an All-Electric Restaurant.

Electric ovens had drawbacks. They needed pre-heating for 30 minutes. You had to invest in heavy flat-bottomed pans for them, rather than the new, light aluminium saucepans. But the smaller electric cooking machines which fried or boiled didn't have these disadvantages. They were a masterstroke of marketing, an affordable extra for people who wanted a taste of the new fuel, but weren't daring enough to replace their coal range with an unknown electric cooker.

The plug-in electric cooking dishes were delectably pretty. Who could resist a silver electric 'chafing dish', which you could use to wow your friends at table by cooking an omelette absolutely fresh. Such electrical extras were an excellent way of keeping cook sweet by saving her work. When servants were a dim memory, after the 1914–18 war, a lady could look serene at breakfast, serving coffee or kippers heated on Belling boiling rings, introduced in 1915, or the Simplex Breakfast Cooker – a table-top kitchenette with a stove, kettle and steel pan with attractive ebony handles.

Some of these meals had to be eaten in the dark. Electricity providers had a two-tiered charge system: a fixed monthly tariff for lighting, and a pay-per-unit tariff for cooking. So people plugged cookers into a lightswitch and didn't go to the expense of installing extra electric points.

Naturally, electric oven makers extolled their virtues over gas ('the only sanitary method of preparing food. Entire absence of fire. Smoke. Smell. Dirt. And most important of all, NO POISONOUS GASES AROUND FOOD WHILE COOKING'). And, as always, people worried. What if it did something nasty and indefinable to their insides? After all, early X-ray researchers died around this time. 'Cakes baked by this apparatus have an indefinable electrical flavour,' was one comment. 'The magnetic forces may enter the food with a deleterious effect upon the digestion,' wrote *John Bull* magazine. The idea that those invisible rays shrank the food was so widespread that the electricity companies had to advertise that it did not.

Apart from luxury and novelty, electricity had an advantage over gas. Gas supplies spluttered and ceased with a change in the wind at the gasworks. Electricity was constant. It was also slow and uncontrollable. Although in 1914, General Electric produced mercury thermostats which gave ovens four reliable-ish heat settings, you had to keep an eye on an oven door thermometer and if it was too hot, open the oven door to cool it. Only in 1931 did electric ovens manage a reliable thermostat when Creda invented the Credastat.

As more power stations were built, the price of electricity fell until most big houses were connected by 1910. Britain became less smoky:

1 ton of coal at an electricity generating station supplied as much power as 10 tons burned in a single home range. The 1914–18 war made the advantages of electricity clear. Unlike gas, electric generators could be used anywhere. Tricity, set up in 1908, supplied catering equipment for arms factories and field canteens. Afterwards, wartime innovations found their way into ordinary kitchens. Belling designed a lightweight metal cooker for submarines which was sold to the public in 1919 as the 'Modernette'.

Only a million people used electricity in 1920. The connection charge was £20, two months' money for a typist. 'Delightful, certainly, but so expensive,' wrote Adam Gowans-Whyte in *Good Housekeeping* in 1922. 'That is the correct thing to say about electric cooking – so much so that the people who revel quite comfortably in Rolls-Royces and piano-players and all the out-and-out luxuries of life will feel that they cannot face the extravagance of cooking their food by electricity.' Then electricity prices dropped by three-quarters. Wartime weapons research had developed automatic timers which enabled on and off switches to be pre-set, and electric cookers incorporated them. 'Leave the Phantom Maid in charge,' urged a 1929 advertisement for Hotpoint, wistfully referring to the service-packed past. 'Play golf, go bathing – enjoy yourself as you will, and leave the kitchen! For Hotpoint's super-automatic controls will watch the cooking as well as if you were there.' It's a great vision,

A G.E.C. PRODUCT

MAGNET

ELECTRIC COOKERS

MAGNET Electric Cookers provide the most up-to-date and reliable form of cooking. Efficient, safe, roomy, convenient and clean, MAGNET Cookers preserve food values, adding a new zest and enjoyment to meals. Cooking with a MAGNET is simple, straightforward and care-free. Economical, too, whatever the size of your household, for there are models to satisfy all needs. A product of The General Electric Co. Ltd., the largest British Electrical Manufacturing Organisation in the Empire. Write to the address below for Folder DC 6442 P which gives full particulars — sent post free on request.

G.E.C. BRITISH MADE QUALITY PRODUCTS

THE GENERAL ELECTRIC CO., LTD. *Head Office and Public Showrooms: Magnet House, Kingsway, London, W.C.2*
Branches throughout Great Britain and in all principal markets of the world.

but one can't help wondering how many women understood the timers enough to use them. How many of us do today?

But they were a sign that times had changed. Thoroughly Modern Millie wanted to party. The Great War had shown her that life was too short to polish a range with black-lead. Porcelain and vitreous enamel, developed in the 1850s, were used to coat electric ovens in colourful, wipe-clean mottled finishes. The newest ranges changed their look, to resemble writing-tables with graceful arched legs. They had convenient eye-level ovens with drop-down doors, next to a table carrying four solid hobs. A slot at the side held the precious cookery book which came with the oven and suggested complete menus and the cooking time for everything – vital for girls not educated to cook.

As more people switched to electricity, smaller, cheaper cookers came out. They were called after London's newly-built outer suburbs. Revo Superspeed's 'Croydon' was the first cooker with hobs which glowed red-hot. The idea of Croydon as a place to aspire to seems comical. But there was a lot of pride in Metroland. It was the promised land in which gardens were large, roads wide and houses modern, the forward-looking lifestyle which people felt their lads had fought for in the Great War.

The 1930s were a wonderful experimental time for electricity. People didn't look for nostalgia; they wanted to sweep away the Victorian dust and the war horrors, and be modern. In 1930, a typical cooker like General Electric's Magnet was finished in wipe-down mottled porcelain enamel, with a thermometer on the oven door and a clunky handle. By 1939, the solid hotplate had given way to the familiar coils of covered wire, which twisted to any shape. General Electric brought out the Imperial, a streamlined, steely white monument to Modernism with 'hi-speed calrod heating' which claimed to cook a potful of potatoes in half an inch of water.

New electric kitchen toys appeared from America: the waffle iron, the hot-dog cooker, the popcorn popper. Britain's vital contribution was the electric tea-cosy. The Americans experimented with today's popular combination, the electric oven with gas hobs, and a coal range with an electric oven and boiling plates. In Britain, new portable cookers like the Baby Belling suited the nomadic lifestyles of 'bachelor girls', an independent breed who lived in shared flats rather than with their families. Poorer girls in bedsits could cook precariously with a combined fire-oven 'electric bowl fire' which looked like a silver saucer. To cook, you tilted the fire flat and rested a kettle or pot on its puny bars.

Huge sums were spent on advertising. 'Don't kill your wife with work! Let electricity do it,' proclaimed one poster, issued before anybody realized the

Dont kill your wife with WORK!

Let Electricity do it

WILLESDEN ELECTRICITY DEPT
131 SALUSBURY ROAD. N.W.6

howler. A 1934 promotional film suggests that electricity can mend a marriage. It opens on the exhausted wife, who never sits down to enjoy a meal with her husband because she is slaving over the stove. After she puts a blackened chicken in front of him, he lobs it at the cooker. So she goes for a walk. 'You'll have to pull your socks up, my dear, if you're not to be left behind,' a disembodied, maternal voice-over tells her as she stops by the electricity showroom. So she buys an electric cooker, dons a saucy maid's apron and produces a mixed grill. 'By jingo, delicious, my dear!' is her husband's reaction. The line 'No more matches on the floor' reveals that the culprit wasn't her cooking, but gas.

Electricity was still elite. In 1939, there were one and a half million electric ovens but nine million gas cookers. Dorothy L. Sayers' book *Busman's Honeymoon*, published in 1937, gives us a splendid snapshot of what went on in people's kitchens. Your choice of fuel depended on your class. Electricity was classy; gas for the masses, and paraffin was for those who could afford nothing better. In the book, Lord Peter Wimsey and Harriet Vane marry and move into a Tudor country manor-house. They find antique spit-roasting equipment in the inglenook fireplace, which was abandoned for a mid-Victorian coal range in the kitchen. They get this going, but it smokes. The house's former owner had cooked on paraffin in the 1920s. The charlady Mrs Ruddle cooks with paraffin at home, but longs to trade up to 'a nice gas-oven . . . same as my sister's.' But her sister lives in a town, where the pipes have been laid, and gas hadn't reached rural areas yet. Bunter the butler is suspicious of gas. 'People have been found dead in gas-ovens.' The rich Wimseys don't mention gas.

They plan an electricity plant in the stables. 'I propose to install an open fire and a roasting-spit and live in the baronial manner,' says Peter romantically '... and have the spit turned by electricity. And an electric cooker for the days when we didn't feel so period.'

After World War II, cookers joined in the euphoria by going a playful shade of pink – at least in eye-catching advertising. Hob settings became ridiculously complicated, with 'thrift' or simmer, warm, quarter-hob, half-hob and ultra-high, and the helpful innovation of switches that lit up to show that they were on. In 1958, Hotpoint announced the bewildering 'pushbutton cooking' and 'talking colours'. 'Just choose whatever cooking speed you want for any unit. Then push a Button. A coloured light shows you what unit is on and at what speed.' It's enough to make anyone eat out ...

These complicated consumer come-ons didn't catch on. By the 1960s, cookers had settled down into boring white boxes, the new squared-off look replacing the curves of the fifties. People who had an electric oven did not see it as an exciting fashion item, or a statement about themselves. The smart sixties chick who didn't want to clean the oven could have a new self-cleaning oven like Creda's Autoclean. This had a catalytic lining, a chemical coating on the oven sides which reacted with grease splashes on the side to dissolve them.

Electric cookers needed a Big Idea to capture people's imagination. It came from America. It was the built-in kitchen. Women saw it first on imported American TV shows. The hobs were always separate from the oven, built into 'apron' units like room dividers: social kitchen/living rooms,

where mum could watch the children while cooking, rather than being banished to another room. For electric cooker companies, 'clean' electricity could provide streamlined hobs, the natural mate to seamless kitchen surfaces. The first built-in ovens were traditional white, to go with any bright Formica worksurface. When a pine-fronted country-style kitchen was popularized by Terence Conran's Habitat shops, Carron produced a built-in cooker which was brown, with a bronze smoked glass door. Fashion kitchens were born.

They were helped even more by ceramic hobs, which came to Britain in 1966 fresh from being used for rocket nose-cones by American space research. In 1952, a scientist at Pyrex's Corning Glass Works in America had noticed a 'mistake' on a furnace scrapheap. Intrigued, he took it away, and found that it was as hard as cast iron, but could bear incredibly high or low temperatures. 'The heating elements are concealed beneath a flat white, heat-resistant glass cooking surface,' reported *The Electrical Age* magazine. Ceramic hobs soon became coloured in brown, red or white to match ovens. Unlike a gas hob, they only needed a wipe across with one of the new disposable J-cloths to clean them. Microchip electronics brought hilite ceramic, with a pencil-thin element embedded within the glass. This was popular because the whole hob lit up when it was on, which made it safer.

Built-in kitchens became a fashion accessory, changed more often than the once-in-a-lifetime expectation of the past. Mrs Thatcher came to power in 1979. An economic upturn and the sale of council houses made more people become home-owners. They felt a pride in having a nice kitchen with extras like an electric extractor-fan. As the property market boomed, built-in kitchens became a vital selling point for a home. The less well-off borrowed thousands to install them in do-it-yourself flatpack form from warehouse shops like MFI. In 1978, a report by *Which?* magazine mentioned a 'computerized' (electronic) oven costing £2,500. It pointed out that built-in cookers gave you the extra convenience of eye-level ovens, but at a cost. 'To get the same facilities built-in that you would get from the sort of free-standing cooker that costs around £150 to £225, you would have to buy at least £250 to £350 worth of appliances, than spend at least another £120 or so on units to house them.' It speaks highly of AEG's Regent at a costly £275 with a 'Roastamatic' dial for cooking meat. This was an early one-up on cooker timers. You tell the oven the meat weight and how you want it cooked; it calculates the temperature automatically. Moffat's new ceramic hob (at a prohibitive £303) had the very new touch-controls rather than knobs, which it felt were 'too easy to switch on accidentally'.

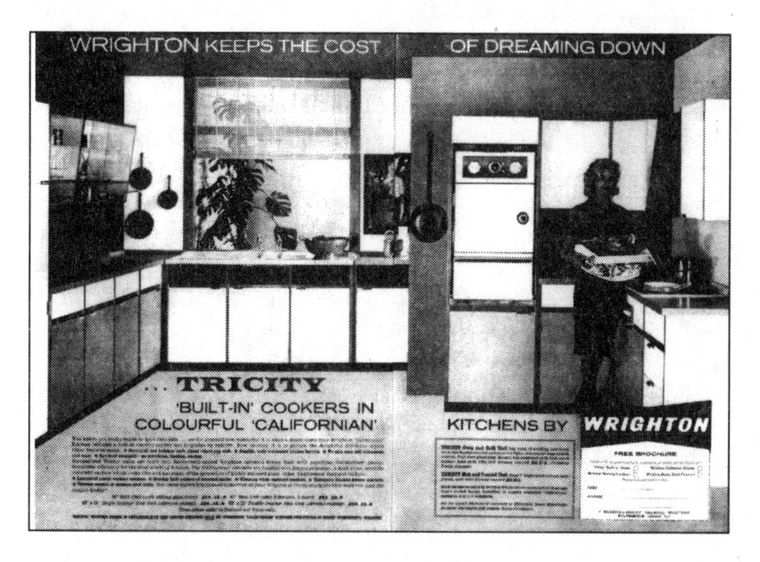

The article doesn't mention fan-assisted ovens, although they had been around since 1969, when Belling introduced them to Europe. Its rival Tricity was developing a similar oven and rushed to launch it at the Ideal Home Show that year, when it heard of Belling's. The idea was simple. At the back of the oven was a central fan, which forced the hot air to move around rather than rising and staying at the top, so the oven stayed at the same heat throughout. Fan-assisted ovens were said to save time and electricity, shrink the meat less and keep the oven cleaner, although some owners found that the fan splashed fat around. They appealed to the new freezer-owners. Keen on economy and back-to-the-land values, they harvested their own fruit and vegetables at the new pick-your-own fruit and vegetable farms, then used the even heat generated by fan-assisted ovens to batch-cook large amounts for the freezer.

European companies, with their smart, streamlined designs, flooded into Britain after we joined the European Community in 1972. We holidayed abroad and saw desirable kitchens there. None more than those of a German company, Neff. Neff transformed the white oven by giving it a dark glass front to make it a symbol of the era. Neff's fan-assisted ovens were dubbed 'Circotherm', a name with the perfect degree of scientific-sounding magic. Slick adverts spread the message that they needed no pre-heating, and saved 15 to 20 minutes of cooking time. 'The flavours never mingle . . . unlike ordinary fan ovens, it's possible to grill on all three shelves at once.' For the first time, cookers were advertised not for 'thrift settings' but with a swagger to a new kind of buyer, who wanted to show off their new wealth: 'from £300 to well over £1000'. Its 'features' included a personal cookery lesson at home. 'Fan-assisted made a difference,' recalls Prue Leith, founder of Leith's Cookery School. 'I had a brilliant oven, a Neff, in the early 1970s that made cooking 10 per cent faster.'

By the 1980s, Neff dominated. 'The 1980s was the age of the electric oven,' assesses Cotswold property developer Ian Simpson. 'Always built-in. Mostly Neff because they had the name at the time, they were what people expected. They loved lots of knobs. But one drawback was that people found you couldn't use the grill and oven simultaneously because the grill was at the top of the oven. Then in 1982, people wanted fan-assisted ovens. These were too noisy. They went on going 15 minutes after you'd finished cooking and disturbed the meal in the kitchen.'

Now people wanted a hob-cum-cooking pot. 'In 1982 I tried built-in chip pan fryers and gave that up after the house nearly burned down.' Another fad was for a barbecue-style steak griller in 1984. 'Men liked those. That soon went out because they were messy to clean and meat-eating became less popular.' Ian didn't install ceramic hobs until the mid-1980s. 'Before that, they were too pricey; we introduced them around 1984 and still use them because they're clean. Halogen hobs came in just after ceramic. Very gimmicky; very quick. People liked them and still do because you can see they're on instantly. They're clean and pretty.'

Halogen hobs were the idea of Kenwood when it was part of Thorn EMI. Instead of a hot element, they cooked by the hot light of the new tungsten halogen lamps. They heated up superfast and looked space-agey, with a bright orange light, but they were expensive. They also suited the newest trend, minimalism, whose prophet is Gaggenhau, another Germany company. Designed by Swedish cult hi-fi firm Bang and Olufsen, Gaggenhau's cookers are described by its UK Managing Director Richard Stone as 'a semi-industrial very modern-looking stainless steel range that wouldn't go well with the country look.' 'Integrated' replaced 'built-in' as a buzzword. In the ideal shiny sweep of empty kitchen surface, which is minimalist home heaven, there is a built-in wok and an electric grill with lavastone griddle plates. Instead of catalytic oven-liners is a pyrolytic oven cleaner, developed in 1978. This heats the oven to 485 degrees centigrade, a temperature which burns off stains, but leaves the oven door cool to touch while it does it.

The latest electric hobs cook by induction, a new energy-mean system which needs special iron saucepans. When a pan touches the hob surface, a powerful electro-magnet makes the bottom of the cooking pan hot, but the hob stays cool. Ovens will become even more streamlined when voice-command banishes controls to a concealed emergency-section. Sensors will detect burning and switch the heat off. Sun Micro-Systems is developing software that can be used for cooking on command. CD-Rom cookbooks are already here. When you wonder, out loud, what to eat tonight, a built-in cooker computer will suggest dishes and talk you through the recipes step-by-step; or even conjure up a virtual reality cooking teacher, standing in your kitchen like a genie. In the near future, cookers will recognize you, cook steaks to your taste or adjust their cooking methods to take account of your weight, or your latest diet.

Baked Potatoes and Burnt Poodles

In the 1920s, the science fiction of H.G. Wells inspired companies to look for death-rays which would knock enemy aircraft out of the skies. Over the next decade, British scientists experimenting with radio frequencies found that short wavelengths can bounce back from objects like ships and produce a radio echo. This could be used to track moving objects on the seas and in the sky – and it became radar, which uses very short radio waves called microwaves. At the start of the Second World War in 1940, H.A.H. Boot and J.R. Randall at Birmingham University invented the magnetron, a microwave generator a thousand times stronger than anything else, which made radar accurate and portable enough to fly in planes as they chased deadly German submarines. The magnetron was our vital secret weapon, flown to

America to be mass-produced by the Raytheon Company, whose name means 'Ray of the Gods'.

It might have been a cold cup of cocoa. Or a chocolate bar. Stories vary, but the fast food revolution was caused by a snack carried by radar scientist Percy Spencer as he passed a microwave-generating machine. Suddenly, it got awfully hot. The microwave oven was born.

Spencer and his colleagues put a bag of popcorn in front of the magnetron and watched it dance around. And to convince his board-members that they should make a microwave oven, he directed the magnetron at an egg, with explosive results. As a result, in 1945 Raytheon made a catering-trade microwave oven, and sold the idea of the High Frequency Dielectric Heating Apparatus, as it was called, to other makers. The first microwave oven reached Britain in 1947. The Arctic Cooker by Amana, designed by R.J. Constable, had three controls: 'start', 'stop' and 'light'. A 1959 oven had a cavity the size of today's microwave ovens, but the machinery to work it filled a large cabinet and took four men to carry it. It was sold for professional caterers, who could see the potential of a fast heat which worked by agitating the moisture molecules in food, rather than heating the air around it, so the dish stayed cooler.

A few early ovens found their way into ordinary shops. Sylvia Smith of Bromley, Kent, recalls getting

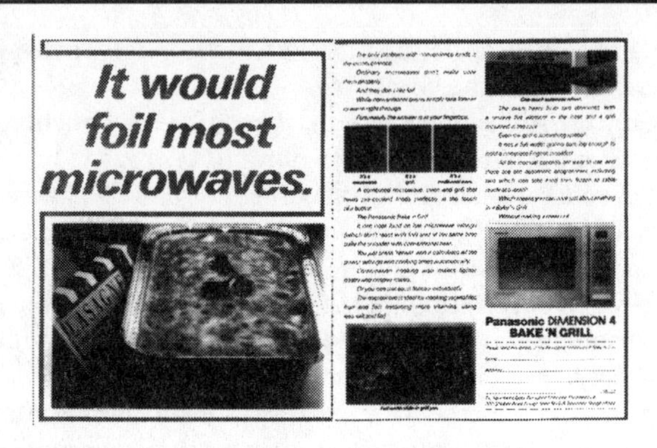

one in the mid-1960s. 'My husband Trevor bought it from Wally Chapman, who ran an electrical shop in Lewisham High Street. Wally knew nothing about it, apart from the fact that it heated his coffee without getting the cup hot. Trevor was fascinated and asked: 'How many have you sold?' 'None,' came the answer. So Trevor offered him a fiver for it. The instructions were in Japanese, so we had to work out what to do. It had no glass on the front, just a wire mesh, and no heat controls, just an on/off switch and a timer in minutes. It was very sturdy stainless steel. Showing it off to his mother, Trevor put an egg in it, which exploded and came through the mesh door, all over her glasses. She thought it had made her blind!'

The first kitchen microwave came from Philips in 1974. Deep-freezer owners recognised that microwaves, with their intense, quick heat, were the perfect partner to defrost the frozen food. The oven was basic for its luxury £300-ish price-tag, with a fifteen-minute timer and a just-acceptable 600 watts of heating power. You could set it on 'cook' or 'defrost' – the same heat as cook, but pulsing on and off.

The new technology appealed to Japanese companies like Sharp and Toshiba. Known for clever hi-fi and computer electronics, microwaves seemed a natural extension of these and their names began to appear in British kitchens. 'It was like a TV set,' recalled Prue Leith of her Sharp microwave oven, bought around 1976. 'We watched it boiling a jug of water and said: "It's amazing! The jug's not hot." Huge entertainment. Things got incinerated, but we were more worried about bits leaking out and frying your brains. I swopped it eventually, because the first microwaves were a bit feeble.' In 1978, Toshiba set out to dominate the market, aiming at the 28 per cent of homes with freezers with The Unfreezer, an oven priced at £199, £100 cheaper than most. This wasn't easy, especially with unemployment at three million that year.

To cook with microwaves needed new skills. No superchef came forward to recommend the new ovens, by now associated with half-cold pub-grub due to a mixture of poor ovens and ignorant staff. So a breed of 'microwave queens', like Jenny Webb of the Electricity Association, toured shows and appeared in magazines, demonstrating how to bake a potato in five minutes and wrapping the new plastic microwave-cooking film over fish. Michael R. Peters stocked Toshiba ovens in his Bedford store. 'My wife demonstrated them to Women's Institutes and knitting circles, but no one bought any ovens,' he remembers. 'People looked at it like you might look at a cobra – fascinated, but staying at a distance. They had this remarkable suspicion. There was always a strong-willed lady at the back who said she'd heard it caused leukaemia, she had an Aga and it would never catch on.'

What publicity loves, it will destroy. On 21 August 1978, ITV's *World in Action* claimed that microwaves were dangerous. 'It came on at 8.30 pm,' Michael Peters recounts. 'And by nine, the microwave was dead. Our orders were

all cancelled next morning. You couldn't give a microwave away. It wasn't what it said. It was what you *thought* it said. One woman went blind and according to them, it was definitely microwaves.' As makers launched writs in America, and politicians reassured the public, the climate of suspicion lingered. After writing a film about microwave cooking at that time, this author was (wrongly) told by the microwave company's own engineer that the oven would make her infertile. That was one of many notions caused by the old idea that microwaves were death-rays, and would leak from a poorly-sealed door into people's bodies. Another misunderstanding, that microwaves cook from the inside out, gave rise to the urban myth of the woman who popped her poodle in the microwave to dry it out, and cooked its innards.

Microwave makers and sellers are convinced that safety scares depressed sales for five years. But in 1979, *Which?* magazine felt they were popular enough to feature for the first time. Although under one per cent of the population had a microwave, it found a sample of over two hundred users, mostly happy. There were also eleven makes of microwave, from AEG's expensive one with a temperature probe to check the food was cooked, to Tricity's £150 basic. Sharp and Toshiba had taken the lead, both producing cheap ovens with prominent safety assurances, and a cookbook promising 'ambitious dishes' to the fainthearted. One of the main drawbacks to sales was down to oven-makers to correct. Microwaved food was not evenly heated. Toshiba solved this with the Deltawave, a glass turntable which turned the dishes so that the microwaves could reach every part. That quickly became standard.

Despite the massive 'education' in magazines about what microwaves could and couldn't do, *Which?* found it necessary to warn that 'most people would want a conventional cooker too – the microwave oven is not a perfect replacement.' Too right. Meat didn't brown without being peppered farcically with paprika to disguise its paleness, or being put on an expensive 'browning dish'. Turntables limited the oven space to one dish at a time. Recipe books were bewildering lists of cooking times and settings, with little or no description of how to prepare the food. One major company was so slapdash that it revolted English cooks with a recipe for an Italian favourite, baked dormice.

Unlike gas or electricity, microwaves were never considered stylish or interesting by top chefs. They were publicly scorned, but useful, shameful secrets in restaurant kitchens. But for families, they made life bearable during the 1980s recession. More women worked to pay skyrocketing mortgages, or after divorce, and they relied on frozen food, reheated quickly by microwave, to feed the family, now that longer hours and a fashion for gyms after work made sit-down-together meals a fading memory. In 1985, 14 per cent of homes had a microwave. This rose to 44 per cent in 1988.

Without the microwave oven, there would have been no fast food revolution. This was really a return to our medieval habits of eating out at takeaways, or bringing home pre-prepared food. But frozen meals weren't the ideal partners for microwave ovens. Aluminium freezer foil damaged the magnetron, so food had to be dug out of the container and defrosted on plates until it lost its shape. The standard of convenience food rose after more imaginative, chilled, complete meals in plastic trays appeared, which needed no defrosting and could be cooked on a plate in five minutes. By 1986, these made up £115 million of supermarket takings, and the search for novelty and sophistication encouraged supermarkets to offer more adventurous meals. The lasagne was superseded by complete Chinese dinners, Indian curries and Mexican fajitas.

Today's ovens are more powerful, slimmer and half the weight. Because of their male-orientated electronics background, they suffer from the common modern machine problem of confusing people with over-complicated settings. One oven advertised 99 power levels and 93 timings. But that same electronics input made microwaves the first home machines with 'smart' electronics. In the mid-1980s, ovens offered to do the cooking for you – exactly as gas Regulos had advertised in the 1920s, but more so. There were automatic settings for popular meals like lasagne, or sensors which weighed food and calculated the cooking time. Sharp's latest LogiCook oven boasts a humidity sensor which 'works out what kind of ready meal it's cooking, selects the correct power level, calculates the cooking time and heats it to perfection. All you have to do is place the ready meal in the oven.'

Microwaves have become tabletop versions of conventional ovens, offering extra alternative heat like halogen, to grill or bake food. In 1987, Creda launched a full-size electric oven which could also heat by microwave. This was a bridge too far for most people. But the move towards uncluttered work surfaces makes this likely to be the space-saving shape of ovens to come.

The ones that got away . . . Paraffin Cookers

After the discovery of oil in Pennsylvania in 1859, the first oil (paraffin) cookers were developed around 1871 by The Albion Lamp Company of Birmingham. Early stoves looked rather grand, and were bought by women whose coal-burning ranges made the kitchen too hot in the summer. An advertisement for Rippingale's Oil Cooking Stoves shows a jolly couple of servants bending over a cooker like a sideboard with long cabriole legs, and a boxy oven at eye-level with four burners, very like a built-in hob, next to it. The oil reserve was stowed neatly underneath. It was a brilliant design, 'borrowed' by 1920s gas ranges.

But oil cookers were smoky and despite the flue which removed the smoke to the chimney, they produced 'eye-smarting smoke and disagreeable odour of unburned oil', as one advertisement put it. Manufacturers tried to solve the problems. Florence stoves boasted 'no smoky wick to trim', a reference to the tiresome stringy wick, the burner whose burnt bit you had to cut off each time you used it. The 1921 New Perfection claimed a 'long blue chimney' which 'drives the heat right through the pan and straight into the hardest-hearted potato' which sounds scary.

Cheaper than coal, with no connection charge, paraffin was ideal for the poorest homes. When mother worked and couldn't tend a coal stove, and families got home hungry after a long working day, it was instantly lit and warmed a room quickly. In 1937, the year of the first modern-looking white gas cooker, Littlewoods sold a very basic oil cooker which looked as if it was from another era, a formalised version of the improvised arrangements of the past. It was a room heater which you stood underneath a tin box on legs to heat it up, giving an 'oven'.

Useful to country cooks who were not connected to gas and electricity, paraffin ovens faded away in a wisp of blue smoke after the Second World War.

Money, sex and broken china

A Victorian photographer called Arthur Mumby secretly married his maid-of-all-work, Hannah Cullwick. In 1879, he photographed her standing over a wooden tub made of a sawn-in-half barrel, with a tiny water jug and a rinsing basin. This was how most people washed up. In those pre-Fairy Liquid days, they might put slithers of leftover Lifebuoy soap in a wire cage on a handle, and swoosh it through the water.

Before that, people ate the washing-up. They used trenchers, specially-baked flat split loaves, as plates. Those with wooden or pewter platters wiped them clean with straw or bran mixed with water, which their pigs finished up. One Yorkshire farmhouse reduced its washing-up by hollowing out areas for each person around the wooden table. Stew was ladled into them and afterwards, the whole table was scrubbed with soda (from salt) and water. Cooking pots might be scoured with sand and salt. Few people had cutlery until Charles II brought back silver from France. People tended to carry a personal knife, fork and spoon with them, and wipe it clean.

Washing-up began in the 1700s, when Josiah Wedgwood introduced new, more affordable ways of making china, and ferried it to the masses via newly-dug canals.

REST AFTER YOUR MEALS

Nothing is more disagreeable than to be confronted with the miserable task of washing-up after a good meal. The preparation of a meal is irksome enough, but this sequel is worse. It spoils the satisfaction of an appeased appetite and sets a culminating seal of fatigue to household labour.

No More Odious Washing-up

need ever worry you if you take advantage of this greatest household labour-saver of all Time.

THE POLLIWASHUP MACHINE

is a portable appliance, entirely free from mechanical complications, and requiring no attachments, which does this unpleasant work for you, perfectly, without breakages, mess, or extra cost.

It requires the simple addition of hot soapy water, a few turns of the handle, a second supply of water for sterile rinsing and the work is done.

Perfectly safe to use and easy to operate. The apparatus is fool-proof, and considerate housewives will install one for lightening the maid's duties.

(Power-drawn models of any capacity for large catering institutions)

Write Now to—

The WASHING-UP MACHINE Co. Ltd.
34 Fulham Road, London, S.W.3

There was an explosion in tea-sets when the tea-tax was reduced from 119 per cent to 12 per cent in 1784. Sparkling china, glass and silver became crucial to the rising middle classes. An aristocrat would look at the dinner table before agreeing to marry his daughter into the family. So the 'good china' was washed with soda by the mistress of the house. The butler cleaned the silver cutlery, removing the grease with newspaper and polishing it, or later putting it into a knife-cleaning machine.

The earliest recorded dishwasher was an American adaptation of a washing machine. In 1865, L.A. Alexander put the china in a basket, which revolved in hot water at the turn of a handle. There were others, including the model of 1880 by Benjamin Howe, who claimed it took five minutes to wash a thousand dishes, and an 1890s machine by Mrs Cochran of Indiana, which forced water over dishes at the turn of a handle.

Dishwashers only got going with 'electricity, the good fairy' as one apostle called it. The good fairy's best machines were French. Since Victorian gents by the hundred slipped off to Paris for a spot of can-can and cuisine, restaurants were interested in any labour-saving device. In 1885, a Paris restaurant used Eugene Daguin's magnificent wheel-shaped dishwasher. It was a glorified washing-up bowl. Eight dishes at a time were stacked inside the wheel, which turned them through a hot bath where two rotating brushes scoured them. Then it turned them into a cold rinsing bath and shook them to get the grease off. An even more complicated 1906 French invention used an overhead railway to line up baskets of dishes over a hot and a cold tank of water, and then plunged them into it.

Without today's abrasive dishwashing powders, dishwashers had to boil water to clean the dishes properly. The British Cornhill used boiling water 'filtered and forced over the dishes repeatedly with great speed, thoroughly washing them in half a minute,' though it used the same water 'for two or three hours'. By which time, even the pigs wouldn't have it.

By 1910, there was a small choice of household dishwashers. 'I advise the washing-up to be done only once a day, and by means of a "Dreadnought" machine', writes Lilly Frazer in *First Aid to the Servantless*, her 1913 domestic manual. She says that the machine will 'definitely wash, rinse and dry all plates, dishes, cups, silver and scrub out all saucepans, in one single operation'. This paragon cleans itself too. The Dreadnought and the slightly later Polliwashup were wooden or metal boxes containing a metal wire basket for the dishes. You added hot water and soap, closed it, then turned the handle to send the water swooshing over the dishes. For families of 10, Polliwashup offered a 10-guinea model 'with gas ring for applying heat, and automatic scrubber for saucepans'.

The Premier Washerup, also 10 guineas, was what you might call passive. It was a kitchen cabinet connected to your sink hot tap by a removable rubber hose, and seems to have relied on the power of hot water spraying. 'Requires no motive power, no preparation and no cleaning or clearing up . . . portable and requires no fixing,' advertised its sellers, James & Copeland of London.

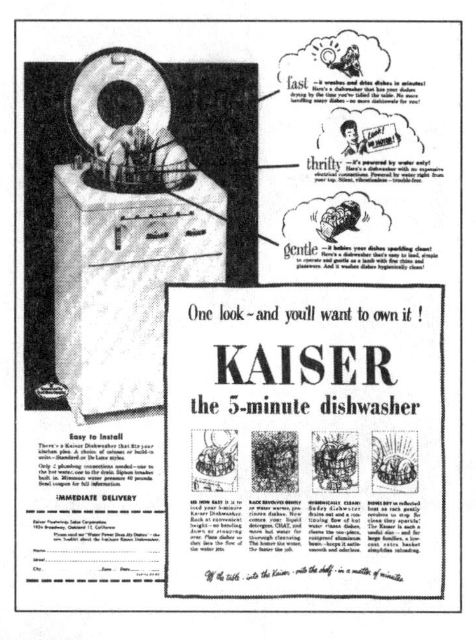

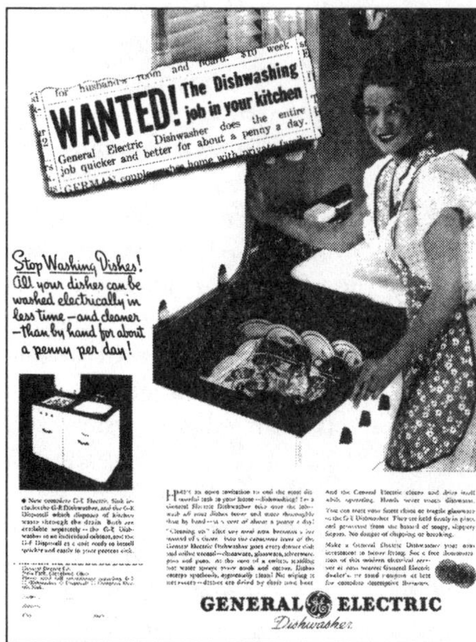

The machines cracked the china, streaked glasses and created extra work which took as long as washing up by hand: boiling water, filling and emptying, loading and unloading. Pots had to be pre-soaked and the machine cleaned afterwards. This was a problem which lasted. Even in the 1960s, an Indesit machine-owner meticulously 'pre-washed'

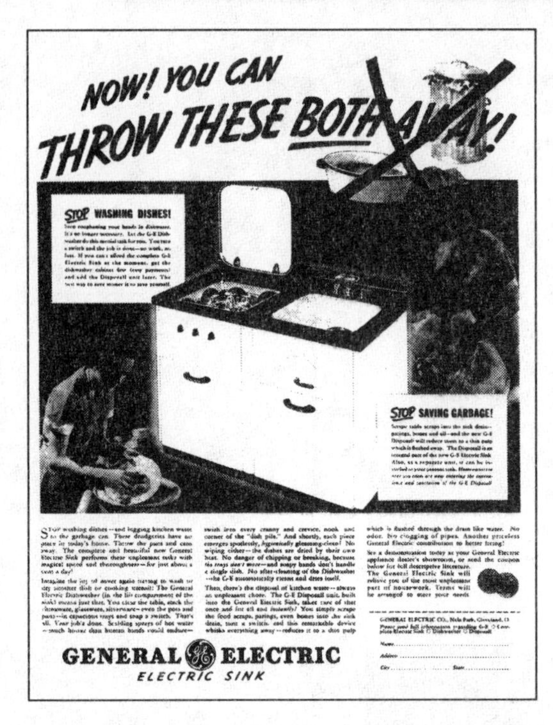

plates before putting them in the machine to stop food clogging the mesh drainer.

House and Garden magazine in 1923 suggested that rather than a machine, one should use a short rubber shower hose, slipped over the hot tap, with a hand-controlled soap dispenser in the nozzle. This was one of the early good ideas that we have lost, like the Kaiser five-minute washer, which had a top-loading basket which sprang up as you opened the lid. You could buy spare baskets to use inside your china cupboards, eliminating the need to unload and load. It was also water-driven: 'silent, vibrationless'.

Space-saving dishwashers appeared. In 1922, The Western Electric Dishwasher and Kitchen Table was a top-loading wooden box which swooshed water around a bit. 'Just put the dishes in . . . and pour in some hot water.' By the early 1930s, the all-conquering General Electric had produced the wonderful Electric Sink. Aimed at Americans living in small city apartments, it looked like a twin-tub washing machine, years before that had been invented. One side had a top-loading dishwasher; the other, a sink with a built-in kitchen waste grinder, the Disposall, which chomped up everything – 'even bones' – to wash down the

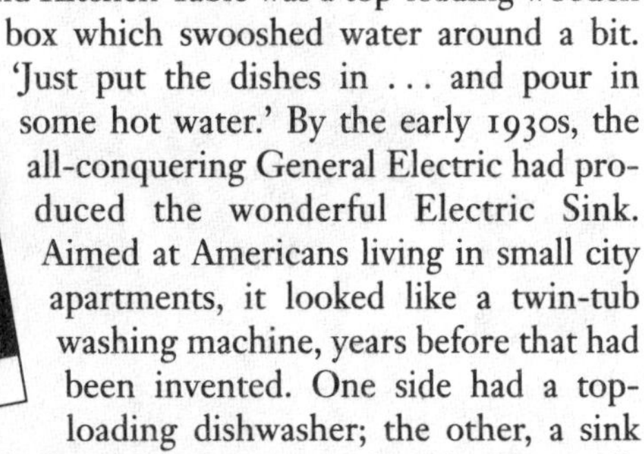

drains, so you could throw away your dustbin (in theory). It was fully automatic. 'At the turn of a switch, scalding hot water sprays every nook and corner ... No wiping is necessary – dishes are dried by their own heat.' The advertising is remarkably modern. 'Upon the startling subject of "Dishwashing and the Death Rate" authorities have pointed out that hand-washed dishes are a major source of spreading mouth-born diseases such as common colds, 'flu and pneumonia.' So you folks without a dishwasher will die, OK?

In 1937, electric dishwashers arrived in Britain. Thor's model combined a washing machine with a dishwasher. After washing clothes, you slipped a wire basket full of dishes over the water agitator inside, added six pints of boiling water and it washed in five minutes with 'THOR WHIRLING WATER-JET ACTION ... Surges water over dishes at assured cleansing speed of 50 feet per second.' The problem was that you then had to drain off the water and all the leftover food bits. But Thor ignored that in favour of a food poisoning scare angle. 'Thor DRIES too – to a SPARKLING finish. No SPOTS, FILM or DEPOSITS, CLEAN – HYGIENIC – SANITARY, because you use boiling water which STERILIZES, and you do NOT use

tea-towels, which however clean they appear to be, are often the means of spreading invisible live organisms on to the cleansed articles.'

There were also cheap portable dishwashers. General Electric's $169.50 drum dishwasher with its 'spray-rub action' held its 100 dishes in a circle like a house of cards. You get the idea that if you removed one, they would all fall down. The Little Friend from the 1939/40 catalogue of R. Cadisch & Sons, at £14 10s, sounds just the thing for those with more money than sense. This was an early plastic machine, 'white cellulose', a mere 17 inches high and 12 inches deep. 'Strong jets of hot water impinge on the crockery and dishes are left perfectly clean and dry.'

In 1948, Hotpoint produced the front-loading dishwasher as we know it, with two water sprays, one at the top. Rather than relying on steam to dry, it used the Calrod electric heating elements it had developed for its cooking hobs. But dishwashers were considered expensive luxuries, even in America, where they weren't available by mail order until the 1950s. Kenwood tried, and failed to establish its dishwasher. British mail-order catalogues carried no dishwashers until the 1980s. Littlewoods offered one 'with built-in water softener' in 1984 at £249.99.

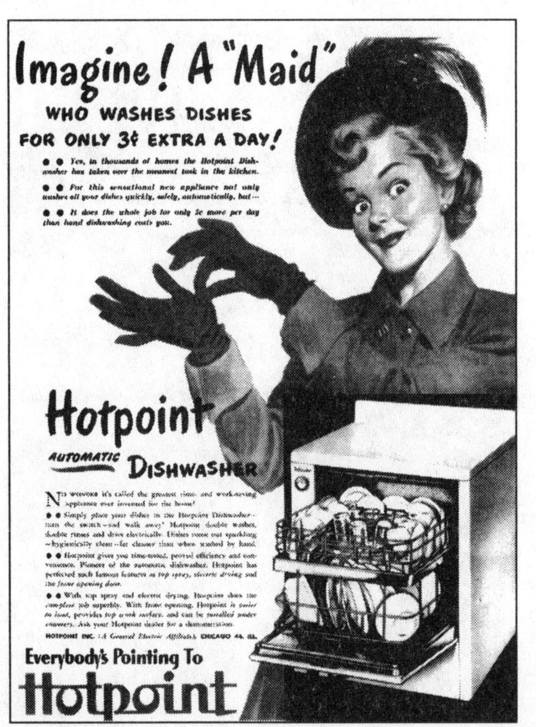

It is hard to explain why we were happy to buy machines to wash clothes or mix cakes, yet to most people a dishwasher was an unacceptable luxury. Alan

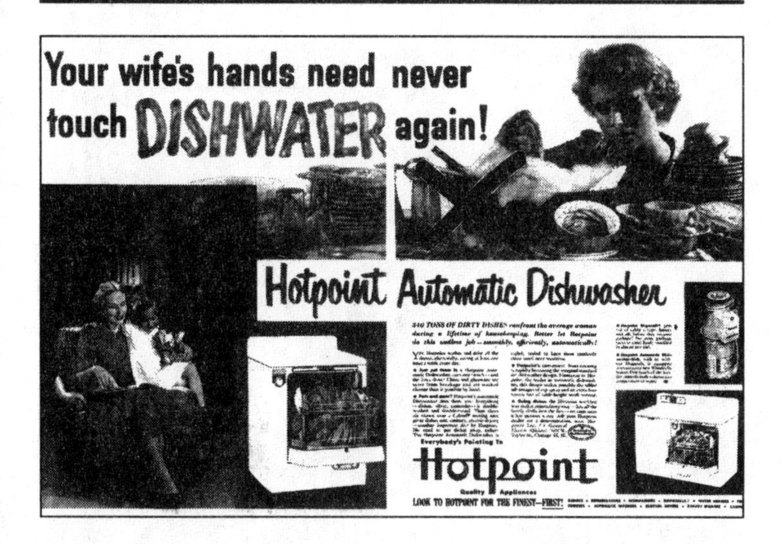

Bennett once wrote of hearing a woman saying that she hated going on holiday because it made her dishcloths stiff as boards when she got back. Dishwashers stayed basically the same, but their advertising tells a fascinating story of our changing priorities. In the early 1960s, Colston imported a tabletop dishwasher. It felt the need to justify its 75 guinea price-tag by suggesting to its audience of proto-Conran types that it would replace your au pair. Then, Miele talked down to housewives. 'A Miele dishwasher is to a woman what a fine car is to her husband. At a quarter or less of the price.' Finally came sex in the 1970s. Dishwashers were the first and only kitchen machines which promised to give their owners more sex if they had them – and advertised directly to men, in the new Sunday colour supplements which they read after washing up the dinner dishes. 'There are better things to do after dinner than the dishes,' said Hoover in 1971 over a picture of a bored couple at the sink.

Prices dropped when Hoover began making dishwashers in Britain. Their efficiency was helped by Lever Brothers' new dishwashing powders in 1966: Sun washing powder and Rinse Aid for shiny glasses. From the space programme came the invention of non-stick surfaces which made machine-cleaning a pan easier.

The dishwasher became a badge of social success as an Aga would be in the 1980s. 'We've done it at last – and what a difference it makes!'

says Mrs Barbara Pattinson of not-very-exclusive Camberwell, South London. 'We've become Dishwasher Owners.'

When home ownership was low, in 1961, less than one per cent of homes had a dishwasher; in 1973, it was only two per cent, around a quarter of a million. But in the 1980s, the swelling numbers of homeowners were encouraged by fitted kitchen designers to fit them as part of a three-piece suite of oven, fridge-freezer and dishwasher. The cost seemed negligible in the overall bills of thousands. It was considered necessary if you hoped to sell your home at a legendary profit.

At the same time, those built-in kitchens became kitchen/diners, and complaints about dishwasher noise flooded in. The result was a new emphasis on quiet engineering offered by German brands: Bosch, AEG, Siemens. AEG justified its high prices in swagger advertising which presented it as a desirable label to have around the home: 'You don't buy a dishwasher just to do the washing-up.' Presumably, it hoped that its more intelligent readers wouldn't ask what else they bought it for.

In the late 1980s, recession followed economic boom and dishwashers linked money-saving with caring. AEG mounted a soapbox on the subject of ecology, reducing its water use to 20 litres of water. 'What you save on water, you also save on electricity. The less electricity we use, the less acid rain falls.' The latest fuzzy logic models pare down power and water-use even more by using fuzzy logic sensors to assess the washing load and how much water and detergent to use. With water an increasingly scarce commodity, dishwashing with sound waves is a possibility. Then again – scientists are also working on self-cleaning dishes.

Everything But the Kitchen Sink

We still use gadgets designed 500 years ago. In the 1400s, they chopped fine herbs with curved, double-handed knives which rocked to and fro in a concave wooden bowl. The Tudors grated cheese and nutmeg with metal graters with a flat back and hand-pierced holes. Cavalier cooks cut crimped pie-edges with a pastry jigger, a little wooden wheel on a handle. They had mince pie tins, oval-shaped to represent Jesus' crib, and heart-shaped cutters to make biscuits, sent not for Valentines but as funeral invitations to those who couldn't read. In the eighteenth century, even more decorative pastry was made with rolling pins printed with carved pictures, as elaborate as a carriage with horses.

The Victorians conquered every kitchen task with cast-iron gadgets, which were often slower than doing the job by hand. In 1864, J. Durrant patented a machine which automatically removed eggs from the water after boiling them. 'Their ends are cracked by being brought against the top of the vessel, a flap falls down to allow escape of steam, and a bell is rung.' Compared to that, A.M. Clarke's egg opener of 1869 seems simple. He just screwed the egg down and opened it with a rotary saw. By 1904, the Germans applied their formidable engineering skills to the matter and came up with the Egg Scissors, handsomely decorated like a cockerel, which snipped off the top of the egg. An American idea was to push a metal 'halo' over the egg top. Pull a lever and spikes shot inwards to yank the top off. But what if your egg was bad? *The Book of the Home*, written in 1900, suggests checking before opening it by putting it in a tin with holes at the top and bottom and holding a gas jet beneath it. An angled mirror would tell you if an opaque spot appeared in the egg shell, betraying its badness.

Before mass-production, food came in unprocessed chunks and needed crushing. Even dogs had their own machine to do this for them, the Rapid Dog Biscuit Breaking machine, with its choice of 'star or tooth rollers'. According to the sellers, Fellows and Bate in Manchester, 'the want of a cheap and efficient machine suitable for breaking up dog biscuits has long been felt.'

Sugar was sold in loaves three feet high and had to be broken up with nippers, which looked like fire-tongs. Raisins made a tooth-breaking mouthful unless de-seeded in a machine like the Enterprise Raisin Stoner of 1895, whose heavy rollers tore off their flesh. The Kidney Bean Shredder's six revolving knives cut beans into dolls' size strips one-eighth of an inch long. And to feed an appetite for marmalade which would have left Paddington Bear gasping, they used the modestly-named New Universal Celebrated Patent Marmalade Machine. 'Owing to the ever-increasing demand for F & B's Marmalade Machines,' warns the catalogue of Fellows and Bate, 'buyers are urged to anticipate their requirements no later than December each year, as the Marmalade Season begins in January and only lasts a few weeks.' These machines didn't actually make marmalade. You fed oranges down a feeder and drew a lever back and forth which pulled a knife across the oranges and shredded them on their way out, so that cook could boil and bottle them.

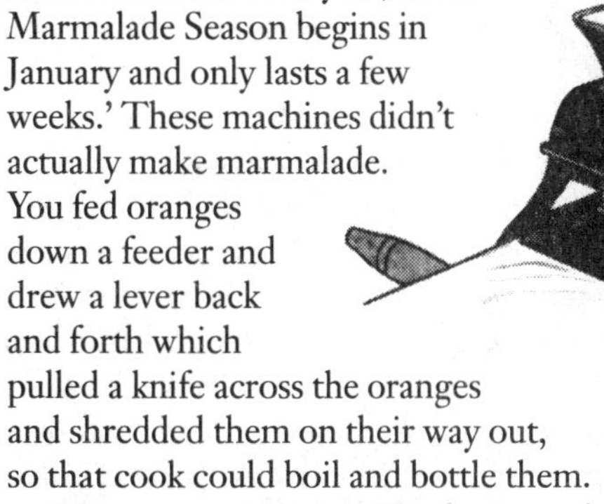

Meat was expensive. To eke it out by crushing gristle in with good meat, you might use the Reliance Silent Sausage Machine

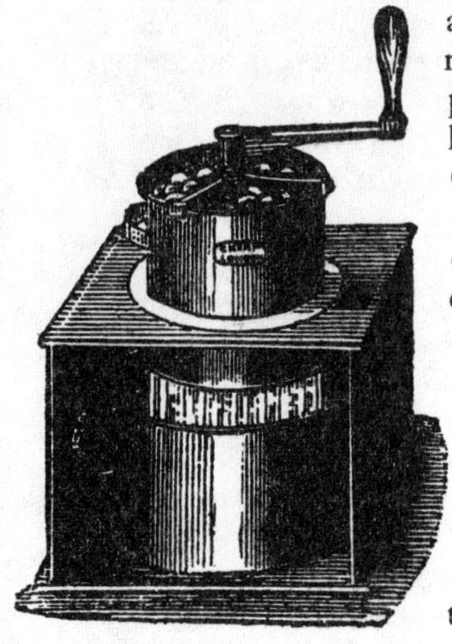

and Pie Meat Cutter, then transfer the result to the Royal Sausage Filler to be piped into animal gut casing. Or you could hide it in a pie made in The Little Champion Rotary Pie Machine. You pushed down a lever on to a circular tin containing pastry and filling and it added a decorative pastry top.

However intricate their insides, all these machines look similar to the Spong table mincer, which appeared in 1880 and is still with us. You feed the food to be processed into a funnel at the top, turn a wheel at the side, and the fruits of your labour are deposited on to the table from an outlet where the machine is clamped.

Goodell's White Mountain sounds romantic. It was actually a potato peeler, one of many automatic fruit and vegetable peelers of 1860 and afterwards which resembled Singer sewing machines, in black japanning, their names in gold on the side, worked by a wheel you turned at one end. The Carlton Potato and Fruit Paring Machine worked on a typical principle. You impaled the fruit on a knife, lined up a blade against it and turned the handle for instant peel 'with a precision not attainable by hand'. The Bonanza Apple Peeler and Corer went one better. Three handle-turns gave you a peeled, cored apple, with the peelings whisked away to a bin at the back. These were the basis of office rotary pencil-sharpeners.

The Rapid Potato Peeler and Washer was a workman-like metal drum with a roughened inside. 'Soak the potatoes for an hour, cover the revolving plate with water, empty the potatoes into the vessel, turn the handle briskly for two or three minutes and the work is quickly done and more easily than is possible by hand,' ran the instructions. Once peeled, you could make the newly-popular chips with the Cottage potato chip cutter. You put a potato on a stand, pushed a handle down and two lattices of sharp knives sprung from underneath and on top, to meet in mid-potato. Or not. Leaving you to ungouge potato from a mass of sharp knives.

Why did they invent so many different machines? The coming of railways inspired a feeling that any bright young man with a Big Idea would rise in the world. 'Build a better mousetrap, and the world will beat a path to your door,' said the American philosopher Emerson. Had he sampled the Uranus Patent Mousetrap? It had a see-through tunnel on a tiny wooden and metal electrified base. Its makers, The Robert Joliffe Trust of Aston Clinton, advised you not to plug it into a light socket, as people tripped over the flex in the dark. You must drop the bait through the hole in the top, then 'place a circle of moist cloth around the trap' so that the mouse pattered in with wet feet, and got a shock.

The coming of electricity brought even more machines to boil eggs. It was hard to boil an egg to order and rush it from basement kitchen to breakfast room. But an electric table-cooker could do that. The Universal catalogue of 1939 includes one. 'Eggs cooked at the table – timed to one's taste'. The instructions run: 'Pour as many teaspoonfuls of water in the cooker as the number of minutes the eggs are to be cooked. Connect the current by pinching together the two buttons at cooker's base. As soon as the eggs are ready to serve the current is automatically disconnected and a small bell rings.' Other experiments with eggs saw inventors putting electrodes in the water to make it live.

Lesser-known advances were the Electric Glue Pot, which stopped glue hardening, and an Electric Sealing Wax Melter. Then there was the Pooteresque 'Cooper's Electric Illuminating Cloth' of 1902. Two layers of green baize tablecloth had electrical wires sandwiched between them with two sharp prongs sticking up in the middle. You hid this under an ordinary tablecloth, ruined by the prongs poking up through it, and slotted the candlestick over them. When the host asked his wife, 'Aren't you going to light the candle, dear?', picture the guests' surprise (or terror) when she pressed the secret 'on' switch . . . and the light comes on without matches.

By 1914, you could lead an all-electric life. Lighting your after-dinner cigar on Siemens' electric cigar lighter (1889), you would recline on electrically heated scatter-cushions described by Maud Lancaster in her *Manual of Electricity in the Service of the Kitchen* (1914). A puzzlingly expert electrician, dotty Maud claims to be 'a housewife' whose jottings are 'feeble efforts of mine to help my sisters in distress'. They would be in distress after following her suggestion for an electrified carpet, before the invention of thermostats to stop overheating. 'A new form of heating element interwoven in a heat-resistant and insulating material (such as asbestos) in the form of a rug . . . imparts a very pleasant warmth to the feet.'

Before central heating, Dowsing's sausage lamp fire, 1895, would be some comfort. But not a lot. It offered the warmth of one lightbulb, but painted orange to give a hot look. And so to bed with the Magnet Electric Bedwarmer, a glazed stoneware hot water 'bottle' which you heated for 15 minutes before unplugging it and putting it in the bed. By the 1930s, electrically heated hot water bottle look-alikes were made from the early hard plastic, Bakelite.

The Bertie Wooster brigade loved a well-pleated Oxford bag, and for that their valets used The Empire Trouser Presser, 1925. It looks like a heated meat cleaver. You squashed the trouser pleat between its two heated metal sides for sharpness you could cut your finger on. This was the age of 'travellers', smart salesmen who sold door-to-door or called on shops in huge 'territories' covered in the new Ford cars packed with their Littlewoods combined trouser and tie press and a GEC travelling iron with a capacious water-filled body which could be boiled as a kettle.

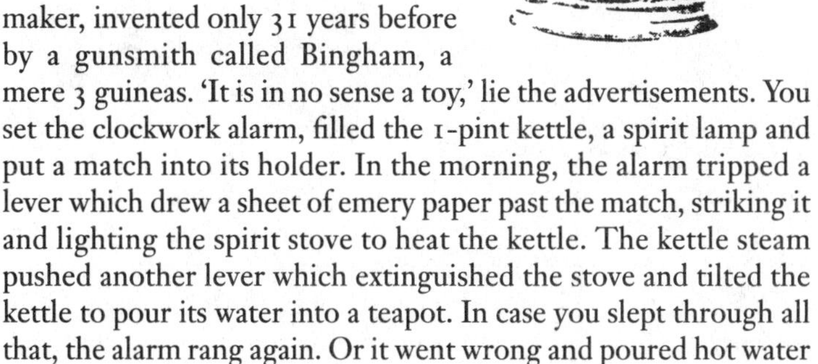

Lack of maids to bring up early morning tea led to the invention of the tea-maker. The Goblin Teasmade in 1933, with electric light, clock, timers and safety devices, was as chalk to cheese from the first tea-maker, invented only 31 years before by a gunsmith called Bingham, a mere 3 guineas. 'It is in no sense a toy,' lie the advertisements. You set the clockwork alarm, filled the 1-pint kettle, a spirit lamp and put a match into its holder. In the morning, the alarm tripped a lever which drew a sheet of emery paper past the match, striking it and lighting the spirit stove to heat the kettle. The kettle steam pushed another lever which extinguished the stove and tilted the kettle to pour its water into a teapot. In case you slept through all that, the alarm rang again. Or it went wrong and poured hot water over the bed.

If you felt weak, you could use John Doyle's Self-Powering Tea Pot, 'no lifting or tipping needed'. You pushed down the plunger, forcing tea up the spout. But for practicality, nothing can surpass Nick Park's 1997 triple-spouted pot which can pour three cups at a time. Unfortunately, this is not in the shops. It was invented for plasticine stars Wallace and Gromit.

At the Touch of a Button

The Victorians had cupboards full of gadgets to whisk, liquidize and chop food. In 1884, a French engineer called Daussin produced a workable engine to run any small kitchen machine from the coal kitchen range. The Lightning, Grafton's rotary hand-whisk, was easy to make into an automatic machine by powering it and adding a stand – a welcome move to cooks when an angel cake recipe demanded eggs to be whisked for 45 minutes.

Other cake-mixers looked like miniature wishing wells, with a handle you turned at the side which cranked a whisk in an overhead section. A powered chopping machine used the same system. A beam over the basin moved a little knife blade up and down inside a slow-revolving container. The problem was, the beam got in the way when you wanted to get the chopped food out, so you had to dismantle the whole contraption – or turn it upside down and risk axle-grease in your apple choppings. There was even a vari-speed chopping machine that turned the tub intermittently or continuously: The American Meat Chopper of 1879.

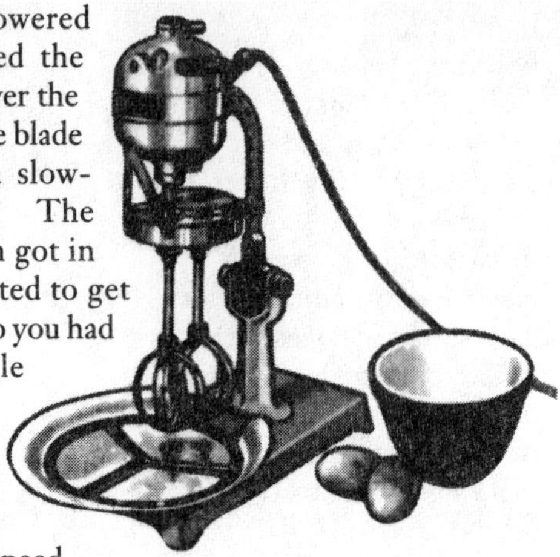

There were specialized machines, like the Three-Minute Bread Maker of 1904, a gold medal-winner from Landers, Frary & Clark in America. This was hand-operated. A tin pail with wire handles, it has a wire dough hook inside, linked to a handle at the top. The instructions on the lid say: 'Put in all liquids first then flour/turn three minutes/raise in pail/after raising, turn until dough forms a ball.'

As for liquidizers, their predecessors were food masticators to help the toothless, old and young. W.E. Gedge's patent masticator of 1874 claimed 'assists digestion, loss of teeth, etc' and was showily shaped like a pair of nutcrackers, the hinged end like mythical beast, with a fish tail and a plumed serpent's head.

Electricity was for the wealthy, and luxury machines came early. In 1911, Siemens produced the Dandy electric fruit press. Three years later, Maud Lancaster recommends the electric Universal Coffee Grinder and Meat Chopper, which sounds like an early food processor. 'Coffee beans subjected to close contact with gas flames naturally absorb some of the unpleasant and perhaps poisonous fumes which accompany gas combustion,' she says pleasantly. 'Whereas when roasted electrically, the process is completed in a pure atmosphere of heated air.' In 1911, the

Hamilton Beach Manufacturing Company, an amalgam of farmhand Chester Beach and cashier L.H. Hamilton, created a motorised malted milk mixer for drugstores, to cash in on a health drink craze. By 1935, American company Waring had produced a motor hidden in a streamlined modern base, driving a tiny bladed liquidizer in a soda fountain, art deco design glass goblet – the 'in' gadget of the smart cocktail-drinking set, driven by anti-alcohol laws in America to disguise alcohol in fruit purées.

Washing machine makers tried to offer better value by making 'powered' kitchen tables with a motor which would drive add-on accessories like bread and cake mixers, egg beaters, meat or coffee grinders, mangle, silver polisher and ice-cream freezer. The Hotpoint-Maytag washing machine of 1927 had a vertical driveshaft at the top of the tank which drove a wringer, knife cleaner, food mincer and a basket for dishwashing. The Magnet Electric Wizard of 1928 washed and wrung clothes, made ice cream and sausages, minced meat, churned butter and cleaned knives. In 1934, Thor's Electric Servant added a rotary iron and a radio for those who wanted to 'listen in' while they worked in the kitchen. Two years later, the Atmos Mechanical Housemaid trumped the lot,

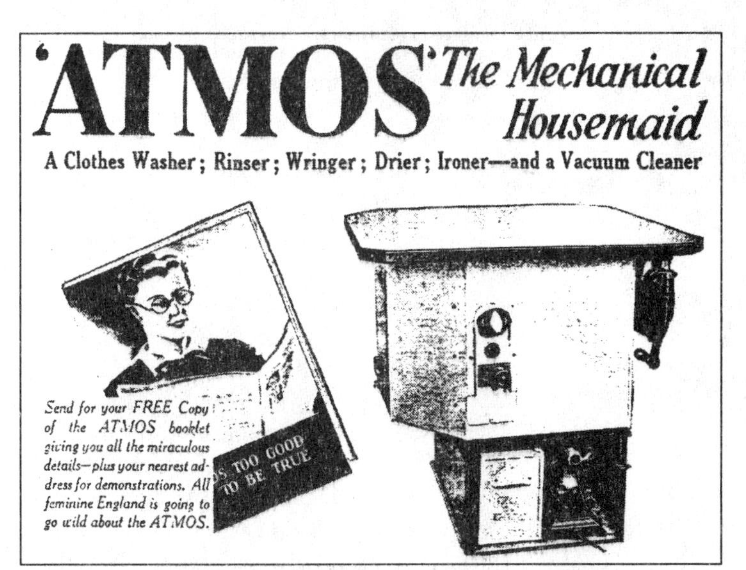

as a clothes washer, rinser, wringer, dryer, iron and vacuum cleaner. There were a few miniature 'electric kitchen tables'. In 1922, the Troy Metal Products Company had a large motor fixed to a stand with a mixing bowl, with a hood overhead which took attachments for coffee-grinding, meat-slicing, mixing, and cutting fruit and vegetables, straining soup, and freezing ice cream. *Good Housekeeping* in 1936 shows pictures of various cake mixers with attachments. They are the ancestors of two hugely-loved kitchen machines: the Kenwood Chef and the Magimix Food Processor.

The Kenwood Chef

Ken Wood, leaving the Merchant Navy after the Second World War, seems an unlikely feminist visionary. He was struck by the change in women after the war. More went out to work, and they wanted labour-saving machines. The sci-fi films of the thirties created a climate of expectation about machines which could do everything 'at the touch of a single switch'. With this idea, Wood devised his Chef with a colleague, Roger Laurence, in 1947, openly using ideas from foreign machines he found in his travels.

As a business idea, it was a stroke of genius. There could always be another attachment to buy, as cooking styles changed: a juice extractor and oil dripper (for mayonnaise), colander and sieve, slicer and shredder, potato peeler, coffee mill and can opener. It would fit in with decor changes because there were five 'gay' colours of nose-cap, cover-cap and control switches to swap.

The Chef was advertised on the well-worn track of the

she's bound to be a good cook–
and save money *too*...
with a *Kenwood* Chef!

No drudgery for *her*—no dull meals for *him*—there's a KENWOOD 'CHEF' in the kitchen! It does *all* the hard work of food preparation, turns complicated recipes into easy everyday delights, makes exciting new drinks and dishes that used never to be possible at home. Peeling, mixing, slicing, mincing, beating, shredding, juice separating, can opening—it's all done in a moment electrically, and far better than by hand. Look at the list of attachments (many of them have several uses) and you'll realise that the 1957 housewife simply cannot do without a KENWOOD 'CHEF', the world's most versatile Food Mixer. *Appointed electrical dealers and department stores stock the 'CHEF' and attractive easy terms are available.*

Note to him! *You can buy her a Kenwood 'Chef' for an initial payment of only £3.15.0 and eight monthly payments of £3.15.0. Cash price £31.8.0.*

Mixing Bowl, taking 6 lbs. of mixture, K Beater, Whisk and Dough Hook are included with every Kenwood 'Chef' as well as Plastic Dust Cover, Rubber Spatula and Recipe & Instruction Book

AFTER-SALES SERVICE

Kenwood Service Engineers call on all CHEF owners twice a year to ensure that their machines are kept in perfect running order. Sign up for Service

YOUR SERVANT, MADAM!

KENWOOD MANUFACTURING CO. LTD · WOKING · SURREY

substitute maid. 'Kenwood. Your Servant Madam.' Although it cost £31 8s, around three weeks' average wages, it sold quickly. This was partly due to superior engineering at a time when Britain was used to shoddy post-war goods, and partly due to an offer of automatic twice-a-year servicing.

By 1956, the company turnover was £1.5 million and every housewife aspired to own a Chef. Elizabeth Kendall in her 1962 manual *House into Home* confesses that she has made a gingham cover for hers.

The Chef was the culinary equivalent of sewing machines that could do fancy embroidery. It influenced a new, fussy style of food in the 1950s and 1960s by allowing women to produce new decorative effects – eggs stuffed with creams, carrots and cress finely shredded, cucumber concertinas. By 1971 it was feeling the pinch. Adverts turned the former 'Servant' into 'Your kitchen slave'. Then came a rival.

The Magimix Food Processor

The Magimix, the original food processor, was the idea of Pierre Verdan, a young salesman for a French catering machine company. As he hawked his wares round hotel kitchens, he realized that chefs didn't need another liquidizer or mixer, but one single machine that performed every function from mixing to making pastry. In 1963, he invented the food processor: one blade in a bowl which could do everything from making pastry to cakes.

The significance of this cannot be underestimated. First, it was sold only to professional cooks. Their experiments led to the birth of *nouvelle cuisine* – a complete change of course for cooking. Food became light, often with layers of pastel mousses, with juice-like sauces beneath meat rather than masking it. 'My first Magimix!' recalls Prue Leith. 'When it came out, it was magic! Why was *nouvelle cuisine* so full of mousses? Because people suddenly had a machine to do them! Food processors changed the look of food. Suddenly, you could make quenelles, sauces, mousseline, without the army of slaves which Escoffier had to strain them through cloths.'

The Magimix for ordinary homes reached Britain in 1974. It sold out, as did 200,000 copies of Marika Hanbury Tenison's

Magimix Cookery Book. 'The reason why Magimix was so successful was that it was so incredibly simple,' assessed John Burgess, Managing Director of Magimix in Britain. 'There were no speed controls. It was geared automatically to add power when it was needed. The only decision to make was whether the mixture was as you wished. It was very fast. You made a pound of pastry in 30 seconds and better, with cold fat from the fridge that didn't touch your hands. This was in direct contrast to the Kenwood Chef – a marvellous machine, but very complicated. If you wanted to mince, you had to get an attachment and put it on.'

Magimix's rivals soon discovered a terrible mistake. Magimix wasn't properly patented. By the end of the 1970s, there were 18 cheaper copies, joined by a Kenwood version in 1982 on the 'if you can't beat them, join them' principle. These me-too machines lacked Magimix's expensive, quiet commercial motor and polycarbonate bowl, a material developed to withstand the faster-than-sound speed of the new plane, Concorde. Eventually, even Magimix produced a cheaper version of itself, Robotchef, at £50 to Magimix's £90. Others, like the French company Moulinex, decided to change the emphasis of the food processor from mixing to chopping, and introduced machines with a separate liquidizer and drum with changeable plates for chopping vegetables.

The Triumph of Fun Over Function

Now people had all-purpose machines, they wanted other machines to do exciting new things. Young couples, affluent without children thanks to the contraceptive pill, wanted fun and dinner parties. They ogled Terence Conran's latest Continental cooking machine in Habitat's mail-order catalogues. Suddenly, food became a way of being fashionable, and cooking fashions changed fast, to fit in with whatever machine was trendy.

Few of these lasted long. Fondue sets inspired dinner-parties to dunk bits of bread on kebab skewers in a pan of melting rubbery Swiss cheese. Chickens were supposed to be more mouthwatering cooked in 'chicken bricks' of terracotta, which gave them a funny taste. Yoghurt-makers and fizzy drinks-makers were time-consuming compared with buying the finished thing from the shops. Deep-fat fryers got dirty.

Slow cookers were a rejigging of an idea first seen in the 1920s when families would go out for Sunday in their new cars, and pre-cook a hot lunch to take, still warm, as a picnic. Those old versions claimed to cook a roast meal for five in separate compartments. The new version was a casserole crock which cooked cheap cuts of meat at pennies' worth of power on a minuscule heat for long hours. The idea appealed to people's pockets, but who wanted to make a casserole at dawn? 'They (the makers) had this theory that everybody was going to get up before going to work, and fry meat before putting it on to cook for hours!' recalled Suzanne Wilkinson, Consumer Editor of the Good Housekeeping Institute.

Another revitalized idea was the heated Hostess tray for meals to be pre-cooked and served to guests by a gracious hostess sitting at table rather than a frazzled cook mostly in the kitchen. Advertised as a new 'way of life', similar hotplates had been around since hostesses first lost their servants in 1914. They needed a lot of pre-planning and choosing food that could be kept without spoiling.

Peter York's 1984 style bible, *Modern Times*, pinned down two new middle class tribes. There were designer-types, who had an exaggerated respect for industrial design. And Babytimers. Their young families gave them a reason to escape back to second childhood and kitchen equipment was part of their grown-up toybox: irrelevant, in amusing bright colours. A favourite machine was the American automatic jelly-bean dispenser, £80-worth of bubblegum machine look-alike containing the cheap sweets popularized by the American President Ronald Reagan. It is their style and their preoccupations that created the kitchen machines we have today.

The Kettle

The most interesting old kettles wouldn't stand on a fire. They had pointed bottoms, and were traditionally used at Cambridge University to anchor firmly among fire-coals without needing a stand. In the eighteenth century, to make and take tea became the core activity of a lady's day. Kettles came out of the kitchens and became showy copper and bamboo tabletop accessories, or rather 'table appointments of striking beauty' as one maker put it, on pretty stands with burners beneath them.

The Carpenter Electric Manufacturing Company produced the first electric kettle in 1891. It was lethal. Like all electrical machines before the 1930s, it wasn't earthed. With no thermostats or automatic off switches, the heating element broke if it boiled dry. Electric elements and water didn't mix well. In 1897, Crompton's put the element outside the kettle, losing the heat into the air and taking an expensive 20 minutes to boil three and a half pints of water.

In 1909, Bauhaus designer Peter Behrens invented the first quickly-boiling kettle for the German company AEG. The element was immersed in the water. By 1911 you could electrify your old kettle by installing a DIY element inside. You could also electrify the water within it. An early jug-shaped kettle, the Hotpoint Electric Jug, presented one of the typical setbacks: if you made tea before unplugging it, it poured electrically live water. In 1916, Lander, Frary & Clark improved this with a plug that melted when the kettle overheated, severing the electricity before the element broke. In 1931, Bulpitt & Sons produced a self-ejecting, resettable plug which didn't melt Bakelite all over the wallpaper. Gradually, kettles became safer, with wooden handles replaced by Bakelite. The Pyramid Wagtail tipped up on its side if there was not enough water in the element, and cut off the electricity.

After World War II, stainless steel and aluminium (popularised by its use in Spitfires) were used in kettles with black plastic handles. At last, in 1954, you could take your eye off the watched pot because a kettle appeared which safely switched itself off. Invented by Bill Russell and Peter Hobbs, when the water boiled, a hole in the kettle lid blew steam on to a metal strip in the kettle handle, which expanded to cut off the power. The Russell Hobbs 'K1' became a British household friend for thirty years.

Teabags and instant coffee changed our kettle design completely. By the 1970s, many people stopped making pots of tea and coffee, and just put a tea-bag or spoonful of Nescafé into a cup. Boiling a full kettle took too long and was wasteful. Kettles needed to change design so that they could boil smaller amounts, faster. Advances in plastics allowed this to happen. Acetal plastics could mould any shape in one piece. Hoover had experimented with plastic kettle lids in 1976, and in 1977, Russell Hobbs used a new plastic called Kemata for the first all-plastic kettle, Futura. Apart from a strange half-handle, it looked like a conventional kettle. Jug kettles were a better design, because their narrower surface area allowed small amounts of water to cover the heating element and heat quicker. In 1979, Redring launched the first polypropylene plastic jug kettle with a useful see-through water window, the Autoboil.

In 1986, Tefal introduced the cordless kettle. The Freeling wasn't really cordless in the sense of today's cordless infra-red computer docking systems, for which you simply put machines close to each other and they work. In cordless kettles, the flex was transferred to a plug-in base unit, and the kettle could be picked up and carried round like cordless telephones.

The latest plastic kettles concentrate on problems caused by hard water calcium deposits around the element: spout strainers hold 'bits' back; Tefal's gold element did not attract calcium; Russell Hobbs' disc technology imprinted a flat element, so there was nothing for calcium to stick to.

In 1982, a small Italian company making ordinary unpowered kettles changed the world. Alessi's kettle cost three times more than plastic kettles. It didn't turn itself off or have new technology. It just whistled. 'When Alessi got into kettles,'

recalled Kerry Daley, Kitchenware Buyer at Liberty, 'they became the style arbitrator and innovator for domestic appliances. People were prepared to spend £60, £70, £80 on a kettle, and it opened the market for others.' The kettle was designed by American Richard Sapper. On the spout, it had a copper whistle, made by the E and B pitch pipes used to tune musical instruments. Reputed to imitate chiming Amtrak trains, Alberto Alessi

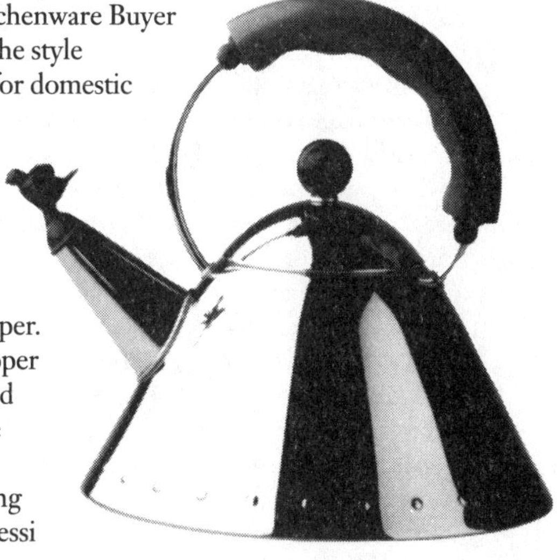

asserts that it was 'inspired by the sound of the steamers and barges that ply the Rhine.' Perhaps it reminded Babytimers of the kettles their mothers had: in 1954, Littlewoods catalogue carries a similar full-bodied electric kettle with 'organ-toned four reed chord alarm'. In 1985, Alessi produced a second kettle: Bird by Michael Graves, with a bird-shaped red whistle in the spout. Even if the whistle became too hot to remove from the spout, it was pretty enough to be pronounced a 'new collectable' with an increasing value. Matching objects appeared, like a sugar jug, designed for display in fashionably bare built-in kitchens.

Electric kettle-makers rushed to copy this friendly, fun look. Kerry Daley recalls the first electric designer kettle by Philips, in 1987. 'It was £59.60 – a lot of money, very dramatic stainless steel with a tiny ball on the end of a short pouring spout.' Where kettles led, other cult kitchen equipment followed, like French designer Philippe Starck's spider-shaped non-powered juice extractor for Alessi, at £40.

Machines had caused many divisions: between supporters of gas and electricity, and open and closed coal ranges. In troubled Britain of the 1980s, Alessi and its followers opened a new divide which was nothing to do with age, class or even money. It was about Taste, and who had it. The majority continued to buy what was in the high street shops: brown kettles with wheatsheaves and flowers on them like Russell Hobbs' 'Country Style'. The organizers of an exhibition called Good Taste, Bad Taste displayed a toaster like this alongside designer appliances, and were accused of tacitly judging people as 'tasteless'. Although they denied it, it gave people the impetus to make new social judgements about people who had the 'wrong' kitchen kit. Designers were somehow on a higher moral plane. The 'tasteful' minority bought expensive, avant garde machines, even if they didn't perform well. In 1990 Philippe Starck, affectionately dubbed 'the designer terrible of our decade' by Alberto Alessi, designed the Hot Bertaa kettle. It sold badly in Britain. Despite the Midas magic of his name, people weren't sure whether the spout was the handle or vice versa.

Alessi's sense of style was taken up by Danish glass company Bodum. In 1993, they took these ideas back to practical electric jug kettles and the mass-market, producing the first coloured plastic kettles, designed for them by Pi Design of Switzerland. The following year, they produced a riot of translucent neons: the 'jelly' colours in blue, orange, yellow, white and green. They were cheap, changeable – and they appealed to a mass middle class. 'People want the fun and fashionable, and they're quite prepared to buy a new kettle in three years,' said Kelly Daley. Suzanne Wilkinson of the Good Housekeeping Institute agreed. 'The reality is that kitchens are fairly bland. Colour is important: that's why we have coloured kitchen appliances.'

1980s style snobbery became 1990s mass taste when Philips asked Alessi to produce a new range of electrical appliances. Others followed. New gadgets like the hand-held liquidizer in bright colours and 'organic' (wiggly) forms have been produced by Zanussi. Who would believe that a Dualit toaster would be produced in pink – and would sell out?

The Toaster

Traditionally, we browned bread against the fire on toasting-forks. Crompton & Co. invented the electric toaster in 1893. It had bare coils of wire behind a wire mesh, which the toast stood against to brown. With its flip-down metal sides, it toasted fingers too. The toast didn't pop up. You had to judge when it was cooked by gingerly opening the hot metal sides, and then turning it over.

Smart breakfast tables immediately adopted this new idea as a better way of making toast instantly, rather than waiting for the servants to trail back from a basement kitchen bearing tepid toast-racks. 'There is no comparison between toast made electrically and that made under a gas grill . . . the latter absorbs the flavour of the gas,' asserted mad Maud Lancaster in 1914. To complete your breakfast table, you also needed a toast crisper, a little electric stove with a hood which kept the toast warm once made.

Toaster makers worked on ways to prevent people burning their fingers. The GEC Magnet had sprung sides so that when you opened them, the bread slid down them and turned itself around to do the other side. The first pop-up toaster appeared in America in 1919. They tended to go wrong, sending flaming toast soaring – or if toast popped out of the back, as some did, it landed in your lap. Most people played safe with do-it-yourself toasters like the 1930 Turnover Toaster by Woodlau Industries. Holes in the frame allowed the first whiff of smoke to reach the user, so they would know when to turn it over. In 1936, the Electrical Association for Women praised a new Hotpoint toaster with glass sides so that you could check your bread's progress.

For all their faults, toasters were always beautifully designed because they were bought to grace the breakfast table. That suited the makers, who hid the ugly coils of wire with imaginative covers, which became bigger to hide thermostat controls and a clock timer like Universal's in 1925, so that toast wouldn't be burned. A 1955 improvement allowed you to specify the toast colour.

The first streamlined moderne toaster, with American bulbous styling in yellow enamel, came to Britain late, from Morphy Richards in 1956. The following year, no other company sold a toaster in Britain. In the 1960s, manufacturing techniques made toasters boxier and less attractive. They paled next to new electrical sandwich-makers.

But another kind of toaster was becoming fashionable, rising on a combined trend for industrial cookers and retro styling. Dualit's founder, Max Gort-Barten, was an aircraft engineer who began making Dual-Light electric fires in 1947. After making a flip-sided toaster, he decided to specialize in commercial cooking aids, like milkshake mixers and the first Commercial Automatic Electric

Toaster. It popped down, not up, to keep the toast warm inside the machine. When chef was ready for it, he pushed it up with a lever. An old-fashioned clockwork timer was used to set toasting times. It was simple, robust, took six slices and had a special slot for crumpets. Toasted sandwiches could be held inside in a 'combi cage', an elaboration of the earliest mesh hand toast-holders.

In the 1980s, Dualit toasters joined the ranks of Aga and Alessi as kitchen icons, displayed in the Design Museum. They cost double the price of Alessi kettles. But their secret was simplicity.

Coffee Makers

Machines to make coffee have the allure of a home chemistry set, making exciting hubble-bubble noises. Count Rumford invented the percolator in 1806 to make large quantities of coffee without the coffee grounds getting in the pot. There were two chambers: water in the outer one, coffee inside. As water boiled, it pushed water through the coffee, then the water sat around the coffee to get stronger. Rumford even invented a 'coffee cosy', which you filled with boiling water to keep the pot hot. This percolator stayed the standard way of making coffee until the 1960s, the most stylish form being the Bialetti stove-top percolator, with its trademark little man on the side. Plain steel percolators percolated to us from America. Littlewoods catalogue carried one in 1965, though a price of over £6 put it on a par with Alessi kettles in the 1980s.

The percolator had too much mystery and not enough drama in its workings to be a massive seller. The Napierian Coffee Machine of 1907 used steam engine know-how. It was a pottery coffee holder with a spirit burner underneath, linked by a glass tube to a glass funnel. The boiling water expanded into steam and was forced up the pipe, through the coffee, and into the glass funnel. The Cona coffee maker of 1910 was the same, but more so. All the processes were visible, through two glass containers, with water in the bottom and coffee in the top. The water was boiled by a spirit lamp underneath, and forced up a pipe through the coffee and into the upper jug. If you removed the spirit lamp shortly after the water started rising, steam expansion would force the rest of the liquid up the spout, and when the steam condensed, the coffee was sucked back down again with a satisfactory gurgle.

In the 1970s, we hankered after the

coffee we had on Continental holidays. Companies like AEG and Braun began producing smart electric filter machines which forced boiled water through coffee in a paper filter into a glass jug. But it quickly cooled and people had no control over the coffee strength. People preferred the simple method they had seen in French restaurants, the cafetière, a brass and glass jug with coffee in the bottom and boiling water in the top. You pushed a metal filter down to force the coffee through the water, and pinned the coffee grounds out of the way. Bodum produced cafetières cheaply in fashionable plastic colours, joined in 1997 by a push-down milk frother for those who wanted cappuccino.

But the Private Gourmets, as Alessi christened its customers, demanded new, more complicated chemistry set coffee machines. Like small steam engines, these are the machines most bought by men, fascinated by their spouts, dials and pressure gauges. They have chugged into modernist kitchens, of all the cult design items, the most precious – especially at exclusive prices like £450, the cost of a Pavani.

The Ones That Got Away . . .

After steam engines came the steam bath. William Flavel, a gunpowder dealer who invented the 'portable' Kitchener coal range, also invented an early sauna called the Vapour Bath, which he sold in 1815 to a Russian nobleman staying in Leamington Spa 'with his family and numerous suite'. When Queen Victoria inspected it in 1851, she was so impressed that her aunt the Duchess of Gloucester ordered one for Kensington Palace.

For humbler homes, Foot's Safety First Folding Bath of 1907 was a cabinet in which you sat while it pumped steam at you. Gas-heated baths, with a gas ring at one end, had been around since 1871, but there were accidents when people fell asleep and got boiled bottoms after they forgot to turn the gas off. For a quick in-and-out bath, the well-showered gent would wear Dr Melchers' Shower Yoke. A larger hands-free version of today's shower hoses, this pushed over the bath taps and sat on the shoulders, where water would trickle down over your body through the holes in the yoke.

Cleaning silver cutlery was a tedious task. For some reason, forks were never fussed over, but knives not used daily had to be

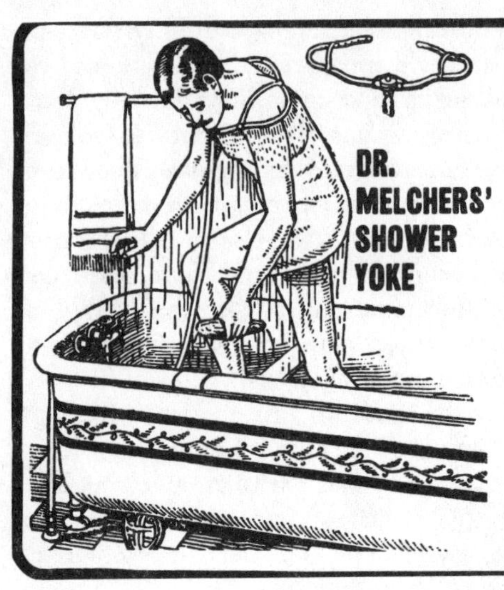

THE pleasure of your bath is trebled by using **Dr. Melchers' Shower Yoke**, which will refresh, reinvigorate, and put new energy into you to an almost incredible degree. You can connect **D . Melchers' Shower Yoke** with any tap, it does not splash or wet your hair, and you can regulate both temperature and pressure of the water at pleasure.

Dr Melchers' Shower Yoke is beautifully constructed and finished, and is sent, carriage paid, anywhere in the United Kingdom for **21/-** for one tap, and **25/-** for two taps. If not all we claim for it, kindly return the Yoke and we will send back your money.

FREE: Applicants forwarding penny stamp for postage can have a valuable little treatise by Dr. EDWARD MELCHERS, entitled "Shower Baths in Health and Sickness." This is worth its weight in gold to all who value their health; it tells you how to become healthy and keep well.

Dr. MELCHERS' SHOWER YOKE CO., Ltd.,
Dept. K.,
3, Golden Square, London, W.

TRADE AND EXPORT.
STOECK, ANDRES & Co.,
19, St. Dunstan's Hill, London, E.C.

rubbed in mutton fat to stop them staining, then stored rolled in brown paper. In 1835, one household manual advised plunging them into earth occasionally to 'sweeten them'.

Knife-cleaning machines appeared around 1884. The American was a simple clamp which you moved up and down over the knife blade. The following year came the Sun, one of the prettiest kitchen gadgets ever made. It was a circular biscuit-tin shaped box with a shining sun picked out on the side. The knives were slotted in at the edge, and emery knife-cleaning powder poured in. When the butler or boots (boot-cleaning boy) turned the handle, leather and felt pads and brushes polished and sharpened the knives. Those left servantless after the Great War didn't have to suffer knife-cleaners for very long. Chromium-plated steel cutlery soon appeared, followed by stainless steel, which was a great luxury in the 1940s.

At Least 20 Different Irons in the Fire

CLEAN clothes were called 'washing'. If they were fancy enough to be ironed, they became the more dignified 'laundry'. Early irons were called 'sad', meaning 'heavy'. Ironing was sad: a hot and dangerous task.

There were different-shaped irons for every job, and more appeared with every new fashion. The Vikings had a mushroom-shaped smoothing iron, which became the glass 'burnisher' to shine linen. Tudor ruffs were flounced against long cylindrical tally (Italian) irons, which looked like small organ pipes heated by having a poker pushed up each one. This became the mechanical goffer or crimper, a construction of tiny heated cylinders which you fed frills through like a mangle.

By Edwardian times, the laundress had a roomful of irons for sleeves, corsets, caps, patterned lace, half-egg-shaped irons for polishing each side of a shirt front, tiny baby-clothes irons and concave hat irons for top hats. All were stored covered in mutton-fat to stop them rusting.

Most were heated next to a fire, covered with soap to stop the soot sticking, which was wiped off before use.

In the 1730s, the hollow box iron appeared. It made ironing quicker because it was kept away from the fire and didn't gather soot. There were two kinds. Slug irons held lumps of iron, pre-heated in the fire then removed with tongs and loaded inside the iron through a flap. When the iron cooled, you loaded a second iron from the fire. Charcoal or coal irons were filled with glowing fuel. If the laundry maid wanted more heat, she pumped air into a hole at the base with a small bellows, sending sparks flying on to the clothes from the chimney at the end of the iron. In 1871, an American, Mrs Potts, invented the first cool handle. Made of walnut, it clipped on to the iron. She sold one handle packed with three irons, so that two could be heated in the fire, and the handle transferred to a hot one when an iron in use got too cold. A little girl's version came out in 1890.

The first electric iron was made for French couture houses in 1882. The Carbon Arc Iron used the principle of light-bulbs: two carbon rods to carry a spluttering electric current between them. But the rods quickly crumbled into white hot ash. A cordless iron, patented in 1883 in America, had no power itself, but was heated on an hot electric stand. In 1889 an electrical iron exploded, killing its inventor. But the electric iron as we know it was invented in 1891 by the British electrical firm Crompton, who adapted a boiling-ring design to heat a sole-plate. Weighing 14 lb (6.4 kg), it was strictly for the electricity enthusiast.

Lighter electric irons appeared from Hotpoint and Westinghouse, like the Prometheus of 1904, but five minutes' ironing used the same electricity as a lamp burning for 69 minutes. After World War 1, the upper classes considered it chic to do a little ladylike electric ironing on newly-invented ironing boards.

In 1922's *Good Housekeeping*, Beryl F. Dupigny suggested of the new electric iron: 'Keep it where you can use it conveniently for your daintiest lawn blouses and the organdie collars and cuffs that are so much in vogue. Allow your maid the luxury of ironing with it in the summer, if no other time during the year. It is surely unnecessary cruelty during hot weather, to use a hot fire to heat irons.'

A lot of thought went into design. In 1920, irons were the first machines to use Bakelite, the primitive plastic developed by Leo Baekeland in 1909, when GEC made it into cool-touch handles and knobs. The invention of thermostats in 1936 prompted streamlined irons with five temperature controls for various fabrics from linen to the newest synthetic 'art silk' which shrivelled under hot irons. HMV launched the beautifully contoured, racy yellow Controlled Heat, with the first modern plastic control knob.

Prices dropped quickly, until by 1939, 52 per cent of homes had an iron like the best-selling Premier Smoothwell. There were rival irons. Methylated spirit or oil-burning irons worked from a little reservoir sticking out from the iron. They were inconvenient and fume-laden. So were gas irons, which had been around since 1880 and had to be connected to a gas lamp. Falk, Stadelmann & Co. advertised The Glide Gas Iron in 1931 at 21s – over double the price of a Littlewoods electric iron which came with its own ironing blanket for use on the kitchen table.

Electric travel irons which heated water for tea and shaving, had been gentlemanly accessories since the 1920s. The steam iron extended the principle, putting water inside the iron and feeding steam through holes in its soleplate. Steam irons came from America in the 1950s. This 'wet' steam heat ironed clothes more thoroughly and saved time: women had previously rolled up damp clothes for a day before ironing them. 1957 was a good year for irons. The iron-tidy, the tubular ironing board, and the latest Morphy Richards steam iron 'with tell-tale light' to say it was on, were all announced in the Littlewoods catalogue. But women

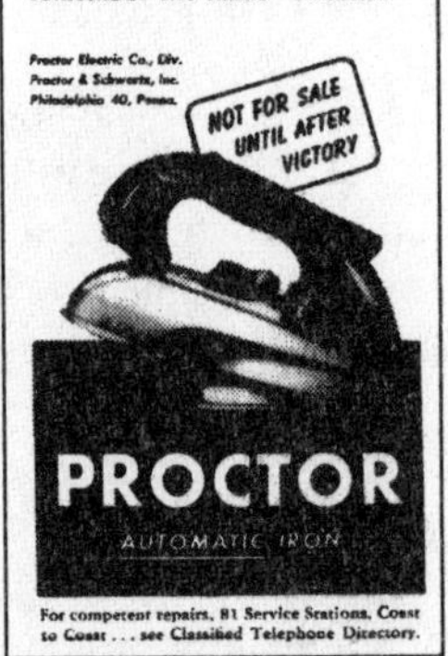

complained that their husbands' new Bri-nylon shirts shrivelled under such heat. In 1965, GEC responded by printing a fabric temperature guide on its new iron. Other fashionable fabrics like jeans were hard to iron. Sunbeam's push down water-spray helped with this.

Through the 1970s, other improvements followed: lighter plastic bodies, transparent water-gauges, right or left-handed flexes, cleanable water-chambers to solve the problem of clogging by hard water, non-stick soleplates, and a revival of cordless irons, heated on an electric base.

The newest irons come from Italy, where snappy dressing is a national industry. They have become 'ironing systems', complicated by plugging the iron into a separate water tank which offers powerful shots of steam. In 1998, De Longhi's twin boiler ironing system claimed to iron clothes hanging up, and reduced ironing time by 20 per cent.

All this comes at a time when chemical advances make ironing lighter work than ever. Synthetic materials 'shrug out' creases. Fabric conditioners coat fibres with a smoothing agent, making them quicker to iron. And Teflon, the non-stick saucepan finish, originally developed as a glue to stick tiles to the outside of the space shuttle, is increasingly sprayed on clothes to make them 'non-iron'.

Ironing ceases to be a task and becomes a pleasure when an electric iron is used

Further Reading

A Woman's Work is Never Done – A History of Housework in the British Isles, 1850-1950, Caroline Davidson, Chatto & Windus, 1982

From Mangle to Microwave – The Mechanization of Household Work, Christina Hardyment, Polity Press, Cambridge 1988

Machines in the Home, Rebecca Weaver and Rodney Dale, The British Library, 1992

The Willing Servants – A history of electricity in the home, Anthony Byers, The Electricity Council, London 1988

Antique Household Gadgets and Appliances, David de Haan, Blandford Press, Poole, Dorset 1977

The Origin of the Vacuum Cleaner, H. Cecil Booth, The Newcomen Society Transactions, Vol XV, 1934–5

Technology in the Home, Doreen Yarwood, Batsford, London 1983

The Housekeeper's Oracle, William Kitchiner, Whittacker, Treacher & Co, London 1829

Mrs Marshall – The Greatest Victorian Ice Cream Maker, Robin Weir, Peter Brears, John Deith, Peter Barham, Smith Settle, W. Yorkshire 1998

The Housewife's ABC, W.S. Fales and J. Hunter, The Modern Publishing Company, London 1921

The English Terraced House, Stefan Muthesius, Yale University Press, New Haven and London 1982.

Through the Looking Glass – A History of Dress from 1860 *to the Present Day*, Elizabeth Wilson and Lou Taylor, BBC Books, London 1989

On the Extravagant Use of Fuel in Cooking Operations, Frederick Edwards, Robert Hardwicke, London 1869

The Cookery of England, Elisabeth Ayrton, Penguin, 1977

Londoners' Larder, Annette Hope, Mainstream Publishing, Edinburgh 1990

The Dream Factory – Alessi since 1921, Alberto Alessi, Electa, Milan 1998

Victorian Inventions, Leonard de Vries, John Murray, London 1991

Illustration Acknowledgements

Illustrations copyright © by The Advertising Archives: pp. 18 (both), 19 (both), 20, 46, 48, 55, 61, 69, 73, 95, 102 (above), 104, 111, 112, 114, 115, 117, 118, 123, 126, 127, 128, 129, 132, 133, 134, 135, 136, 137, 141, 142, 143 (both), 144 (above), 145 (below), 146, 147, 148 (both), 170 (both), 176, 177; Amberley Museum: pp. 16, 35, 40, 43, 68, 105, 125, 140, 144 (below), 145 (above), 165, 168; Birds Eye Wall's Limited: p. 82; Robert Bosch Domestic Appliances Limited: p. 74; Electrolux: p. 22; Forma House Limited: p. 23; Supplied by Kenwood Limited: p. 158; Mary Evans Picture Library: p. 141; Miele: p. 32; Reproduced by permission of Reckitt & Colman Products Limited: p. 98; Advertisement by permission of Vax Ltd: p. 21

Whilst every effort has been made to trace the owners of copyright material, in a few cases this has proved to be problematic and so we take this opportunity to offer our apologies to any copyright holders whose rights we may have unwittingly infringed.